Winter in Eden

When your heart is cold toward God

By Julia Anshasi

Giant Publishing Company
Lincoln, Nebraska, USA

2020 by Julia Anshasi

Published by Giant Publishing Company
Post Office Box 6455
Lincoln, NE 68506
www.giantpublishingcompany.com

Printed in the United States of America

Library of Congress Cataloging-in-Publication Data
Anshasi, Julia, 1963 -
Winter in Eden/Bible Commentary/Julia Anshasi
    1. Christianity
    2. Bible Commentary
TXu 002208001   2020

All scriptures are from the King James Version of the Bible, unless otherwise specified.

ISBN 978-0-9995873-9-3

Books by Julia Anshasi

Broken ~ Poems from the Holy Spirit
Copyright 2017 – Winner of the 2021 Illumination
Book Awards Silver Medal

Some Things are HOT! Some Things are NOT!
Copyright 2018

*Behind the Word: Bible Stories to Ignite Your
Imagination*
Copyright 2018

Why Did the Dinosaurs Die?
Copyright 2019

The Revelation of Jesus Christ
Copyright 2020

One Part Nonsense
Copyright 2020

Spiritual Exhaustion
Copyright 2021 - Winner of the 2022 Illumination
Book Awards Silver Medal

Forgiving Yourself
Copyright 2021

Lame for Life
Copyright 2022

Quiet ~ A devotional
Copyright 2022

Introduction

I've heard many sermons preached on Eden. Invariably the preacher will say something like, "And God actually walked with Adam in the cool of the day; isn't that wonderful?"

Far from being wonderful, it is frightening. This is a misquotation and a misunderstanding of what the scripture says. In Genesis 3:8 we read:

And they heard the voice of the LORD God walking in the garden in the cool of the day: and Adam and his wife hid themselves from the presence of the LORD God...

This occurred after Adam and Eve fell into sin, not before. The human heart is always wandering away from God, and in some cases, deliberately turning away from Him. When our hearts are cold, we are thrust into the "cool of the day," and it is not a wonderful place to be.

When we stay close to God, when we bring our sins and our troubles to Him, our hearts remain warm toward Him, and we enjoy fellowship with Him.

May we all remain in the warmth of His presence. Amen.

Julia Anshasi
Author, Bible teacher, winner of multiple Illumination
Book Awards
2020

For Jennifer
Eden is a beautiful place to be.

Table of Contents

Chapter 1: Eden

How can our very limited human minds comprehend Eden?

And the LORD God planted a garden eastward in Eden; and there he put the man whom he had formed. Genesis 2:8

That one verse could be expounded upon for hours! God Himself, Jehovah Almighty, planted a garden, and put mankind in it. God made a special place for you and me - a place that was free from worry, free from pain, and free from suffering of any kind.

The Bible tells us a little bit about this garden.

And out of the ground made the LORD God to grow every tree that is pleasant to the sight, and good for food; the tree of life also in the midst of the garden, and the tree of knowledge of good and evil. And a river went out of Eden to water the garden; and from thence it was parted, and became into four heads. The name of the first is Pison: that is it which compasseth the whole land of Havilah, where there is gold, and the gold of that land is good: there is bdellium and the onyx stone. And the name of the second river is Gihon: the same is it that compasseth the whole land of Ethiopia. And the name of the third river is Hiddekel: that is it which goeth toward the east of Assyria. And the fourth river is Euphrates. Genesis 2:9-14

God made "every tree that is pleasant to the sight, and good for food." He also made a river to water all the trees.

In many places in the Bible, we read that trees are symbols for believers (Numbers 24:5-6, Judges 9:8-15, 1 Chronicles 16:33, Psalm 1:3, Isaiah 61:3, Zechariah 4:11, Mark 8:24, Revelation 7:1, 8:7, 9:4, 11:4).

We also read that water is a symbol of God's word (Jeremiah 2:13, 17:13, John 4:10, 7:38, Revelation 7:17, 8:10-11). In Eden there were trees, and there was a river to water the trees. This is a symbolic picture of God's intent for the believer - that we would be watered, and thereby grow, from His word.

As I said, our human minds are very limited. When we think of trees that are "good for food," we think of apple trees, orange trees, palm trees, mango trees, etc. I believe the trees in Eden included all of those, plus many, many more varieties that are no longer accessible to us today.

Look at all the trees we have. Oak trees, maple trees, sycamore trees, birch trees, fir trees... None of those produce fruit that people can eat. In Eden, I believe they did. When Adam fell, the creation fell along with him, and trees that once produced abundant fruit began to produce very limitedly, and the trees that today don't bear fruit, did in Eden, and now are barren.

Likewise, many people who are supposed to bear spiritual fruit, have withered from their roots, so to speak, and bear nothing, and the word of God is of no benefit to them, because they have rejected it.

For my people have committed two evils; they have forsaken me the fountain of living waters, and hewed them out cisterns, broken cisterns, that can hold no water. Jeremiah 2:13

What a sad state of affairs.

I can't be dogmatic about this, but I believe the trees in Eden, before the fall, produced every flavor and texture of food (fruit) imaginable. I believe there was an ice cream tree, a pizza tree, a cake tree – you get the idea! We are limited only by our imagination as to what Eden was like and what it contained. But we know from the scripture that it was a perfect place, and the garden provided every possible thing that man could ever need.

And God saw everything that he had made, and, behold, it was very good. Genesis 1:31a

Man had a relationship with God in Eden that he has never had since. Deep within the heart of every human being is a deep longing to "get back to Eden," and get back to the lost relationship that we once had with Him.

Someone may say, "I'm a Christian, and I have Jesus in my heart. What more could I want?" I don't know about you, but this is what I want:

I want to talk to every bird, fish, reptile, and mammal on this planet, and have them understand what I am saying.

I want them to talk to me, and I want to understand what they are saying.

I want to pick up a baby lion and play with it, while its mother lioness rubs up against me and purrs.

I want to entrust my child to the elephant while I go out, and come back to find her asleep in the curve of his trunk, as he has rocked her to sleep.

I want to hear the voice of God Almighty, not in sporadic flashes or brief whispers as I hear it now, but clearly and strongly, every day, in such a way that there is no doubt as to Who is speaking.

I want to reach up and take His hand, and have Him hold my hand, as we walk together.

I want to run barefooted through fields, across rocks, and through the woods, without ever getting a cut, or a thorn or splinter in my foot.

I want to live in a place where there is no longer any miscommunication, where no one hurts anyone, ever, and where there is perfect peace and joy at all times.

That is Eden.

Chapter 2: Created for unity

God created Adam for one reason, and that was to be one with Him. Scripture tells us that Adam had this unity with God, for a short time.

And God said, Let us make man in our image, after our likeness: and let them have dominion over the fish of the sea, and over the fowl of the air, and over the cattle, and over all the earth, and over every creeping thing that creepeth upon the earth. So God created man in his own image, in the image of God created he him; male and female created he them. And God blessed them, and God said unto them, Be fruitful, and multiply, and replenish the earth, and subdue it: and have dominion over the fish of the sea, and over the fowl of the air, and over every living thing that moveth upon the earth. Genesis 1:26-28

God created man, then blessed him and gave him a job to do. What a privilege!

Man had dominion over the animals. Some people get up in arms about this and find it offensive. But God's intention was for man to have the same authority over the animals that He Himself has. Dominion isn't about humans' autocratic rule over or abuse of animals; it's about an agreed-upon relationship of mutual respect. How wonderful it would be to be in Eden and hold that lion cub in my arms, having no fear that its mother would tear me to pieces. She wouldn't, because she would know that I meant no harm to her or her baby. She in fact would be delighted to share her offspring with me, knowing the joy it would bring to me.

Adam had that kind of communication with the animals. God asked them to come to Adam so he could name them, and they came. Nowhere in scripture does it say Adam had to chase down the animals who were running away from him in fear, so he could wrestle them to the ground and name them. No, it was a beautiful, simple process, with perfect communication between Adam and the animals.

And out of the ground the LORD God formed every beast of the field, and every fowl of the air; and brought them unto Adam to see what he would call them: and whatsoever Adam called every living creature, that was the name thereof. And Adam gave names to all cattle, and to the fowl of the air, and to every beast of the field. Genesis 2:19-20a

From God to Adam, then from Adam to the animals. It was a perfect line of communication, with no misunder-standings and no fear.

And the LORD God caused a deep sleep to fall upon Adam, and he slept: and he took one of his ribs, and closed up the flesh instead thereof; And the rib, which the LORD God had taken from man, made he a woman, and brought her unto the man. And Adam said, This is now bone of my bones, and flesh of my flesh: she shall be called Woman, because she was taken out of Man. Therefore shall a man leave his father and his mother, and shall cleave unto his wife: and they shall be one flesh. And they were both naked, the man and his wife, and were not ashamed. Genesis 2:21-25

The word "naked" has a far deeper meaning than simply not wearing any clothing. The first man and woman didn't need to wear physical clothing, because they lived in a perfect environment that was never too hot or cold. Nothing ever scratched them, and no insects ever bit them. But they were also emotionally naked. They had absolutely nothing to hide from God or each other. They lived in perfect unity with God and one another.

For there is nothing covered, that shall not be revealed; neither hid, that shall not be known. Therefore whatsoever ye have spoken in darkness shall be heard in the light; and that which ye have spoken in the ear in closets shall be proclaimed upon the housetops. (Luke 12:2-3)

No matter how much we try to hide from God, He always knows where we are. I don't just mean He knows where we are physically; He also knows where we are mentally, emotionally, spiritually, financially, and in every other way.

For now we see through a glass, darkly; but then face to face: now I know in part; but then shall I know even as also I am known. (1 Corinthians 13:12)

God knows us perfectly, and He is transforming us day by day into the image of Jesus Christ. When we are fully transformed, we will know Him perfectly, in the same way that He knows us.

Jesus prayed for His disciples, shortly before He was crucified. He prayed for unity.

Neither pray I for these alone, but for them also which shall believe on me through their word; That they all may be one; as thou, Father, art in me, and I in thee, that they also may be one in us: that the world may believe that thou hast sent me. And the glory which thou gavest me I have given them; that they may be one, even as we are one: I in them, and thou in me, that they may be made perfect in one; and that the world may know that thou hast sent me, and hast loved them, as thou hast loved me. (John 17:20-23)

I long for that kind of unity; don't you?

Adam had perfect unity with God before the fall. Adam is a type of Christ; in other words, he is an example of the son of God.

And so it is written, The first man Adam was made a living soul; the last Adam was made a quickening spirit. Howbeit that was not first which is spiritual, but that which is natural; and afterward that which is spiritual. The first man is of the earth, earthy; the second man is the Lord from heaven. As is the earthy, such are they also that are earthy: and as is the heavenly, such are they also that are heavenly. And as we have borne the image of the earthy, we shall also bear the image of the heavenly. (1 Corinthians 15:45-49)

In Luke 3 we read of the genealogy of Jesus Christ. It begins with his step-father, Joseph, and goes all the way back to Adam.

And Jesus himself began to be about thirty years of age, being (as was supposed) the son of Joseph, which was the son of Heli, (Luke 3:23)

After Heli is mentioned, seventy more ancestors of Jesus Christ are listed. The genealogy concludes:

Which was the son of Enos, which was the son of Seth, which was the son of Adam, which was the son of God. (Luke 3:38)

Adam was the first son of God. He was made of dirt, to put it bluntly. The Bible describes him as "earthy," which is different from "earthly." Earthy means made of dirt. Earthly means being a part of the world and its systems.

Jesus Christ is the Lord from heaven, as we read in 1 Corinthians 15:47. Both the earthy man and the heavenly man had perfect unity with God, although Adam's was short-lived.

Jesus Christ is the perfect example for you and me of how a man, a human being, can be one with God. Someone may say, "Of course, Jesus is one with God; He's God Himself." And yes, that is true in one sense. But we must remember that Jesus Christ set aside His deity and took on humanity. As you and I put on and take off a jacket, Jesus Christ "took off" His deity and "put on" human flesh. This is why we read in so many places that He went to a place by Himself, to pray and seek God's will. Jesus, the man, could not know God's will unless He sought it, just as you and I cannot know it unless we seek it. Jesus, the Son of God and part of the Godhead, always knew the Father's will, before He "put on" humanity and came to live with us.

Adam knew the Father's will, before the fall, and had perfect oneness with Him. He is also an example for us – an example of what not to do.

Chapter 3: Cold

And the eyes of them both were opened, and they knew that they were naked; and they sewed fig leaves together, and made themselves aprons. And they heard the voice of the LORD *God walking in the garden in the cool of the day: and Adam and his wife hid themselves from the presence of the* LORD *God amongst the trees of the garden. (Genesis 3:7-8)*

Most people are familiar with the sad story of the fall of man. Eve was tricked by Satan into eating the fruit from the one tree that God had told the man not to eat from. Adam then ate the fruit his wife gave him. And their "eyes were opened."

A little child has no self-consciousness. This is why you see little children pulling off their diapers and running out of the house naked. This is why little children blurt out uncomfortable truths to anyone, anywhere, without stopping to weigh their words or use any measure of tact. Before the fall, Adam and Eve had no self-consciousness. They were childlike in their faith and interactions. They never thought there was any problem with being naked, physically or emotionally.

But after they ate the fruit, there was a big problem.

And they heard the voice of the LORD *God walking in the garden in the cool of the day...*

After Adam and Eve sinned, their hearts started to become cold toward God. Instead of running toward God with tears of repentance, they ran away from Him and hid.

What would have happened if they would have stepped out from behind the trees, approached God humbly, and asked for His forgiveness?

But they didn't. God, of course, knew what had happened, and when they finally admitted what they had done, after excuses and blaming, He cursed Satan, the woman, the man, and the ground.

To this very day, hiding and blaming are the natural responses of anyone who sins. Satan lied to Eve, and he lies to us still. Do any of these lies sound familiar to you?

- If I just keep quiet about it, no one will ever know.
- If someone finds out, I'll shift the blame onto someone else.
- It's not really my fault. It's the way I was raised.

Those are the lowest-level lies that Satan uses. But they escalate from there:

- If God really loved you, He wouldn't have allowed you to fall into this sin.
- You've sinned one too many times. He can't forgive you now.
- You've committed the unpardonable sin. You're going to hell.
- You're too dirty, ugly, rotten and sinful for anyone to love you.
- Everyone would be better off if you were dead.

If you believe Satan's lies, you will run and hide from God. You will believe that not even God can help you. Oh, the human mind is so tiny and puny compared to Him! How do you think you can hide from God? Don't you think He knows where you are? God knew where Adam and Eve

17

were, even though He moved through the trees calling, "Where are you?" He wanted them to come forward and confess what they had done.

Don't let your heart grow cold toward God. No matter what sins you've committed, remember this:

If we confess our sins, He is faithful and just to forgive us our sins, and to cleanse us from all unrighteousness (1 John 1:9).

Chapter 4: Warnings

How do you know if your heart is growing cold toward God?

Remember, Satan sets us up to fall. That's one of his favorite things to do. But the Bible says:

For a just man falleth seven times, and riseth up again: but the wicked shall fall into mischief. (Proverbs 24:16)

Warning number one: When you sin (not if), do you run to God? Do you repent before Him with tears? Or, do you make excuses for your sin? Do you say that it's not that big of a deal?

Remember, prior to the fall, Adam and Eve lived in a world with no sin. The sudden realization that they were naked (their sins were exposed) must have been a huge shock to them. They blamed and made excuses.

The more you make excuses for your sin, the colder your heart will become.

Adam and Eve didn't have the Bible to read! They didn't know that they could turn to God and ask Him to forgive them. You and I have no such excuse.

Warning number two: Are you starting to get tired of asking God for certain things? This usually happens when a person has been praying about a certain situation for many months or years. We sometimes reach a point where we tell ourselves, "I'm not going to pray about this anymore." But the Bible says:

And he spake a parable unto them to this end, that men ought always to pray, and not to faint; Saying, There was in a city a judge, which feared not God, neither regarded man: And there was a widow in that city; and she came unto him, saying, Avenge me of mine adversary. And he would not for a while: but afterward he said within himself, Though I fear not God, nor regard man; Yet because this widow troubleth me, I will avenge her, lest by her continual coming she weary me. And the Lord said, Hear what the unjust judge saith. And shall not God avenge his own elect, which cry day and night unto him, though he bear long with them? I tell you that he will avenge them speedily. Nevertheless when the Son of man cometh, shall he find faith on the earth? (Luke 18:1-8)

This is a great mystery of God. I wish I could explain it, but I can't. God expects you and me to "pray without ceasing" (1 Thessalonians 5:17). That means to pray until the prayer is answered.

True, we are only human. We don't have an infinite capacity to wait on God and to patiently endure until our prayers are answered. The natural human tendency is to give up and move on. This is why we must depend on the Holy Spirit to help us to pray. We need to ask Him daily, sometimes hourly, for the strength to keep praying.

I was greatly convicted when I read a book about prayer. In it, there was a story about a woman who prayed for her mother to receive salvation. She prayed for *thirty-five years*. At the end of that time, her mother finally received Christ. The woman was in tears on the day her mother was baptized, because she realized how close she had come to giving up on her.

Don't ever give up on prayer.

Warning number three: Are you complaining?

And when the people complained, it displeased the LORD: and the LORD heard it; and his anger was kindled; and the fire of the LORD burnt among them, and consumed them that were in the uttermost parts of the camp. (Numbers 11:1)

Complaining is dangerous business. The sad thing is, many of us complain and we don't even realize it. I used to live a lifestyle of complaining, and I thought it was just "normal."

The heart is deceitful above all things, and desperately wicked: who can know it? (Jeremiah 17:9)

We are deceiving ourselves when we say that complaining is normal. It is normal in Satan's kingdom, but it is a desperately wicked thing to do for those in God's kingdom.

Have you ever been around someone who constantly complains? Before long, you find yourself complaining right along with that person. The same holds true for gossip. Pretty soon you are joining in the gossip.

The Lord showed me this very plainly. Due to a serious problem in my family, I found myself in overwhelming financial difficulty. I was lying in my bed one night, complaining to the Lord about all the things that I didn't have. I was living in a tiny house and driving an old car. My clothes came from the thrift store. I was getting food out of garbage cans, because after I paid all my bills each month, there was no money left to buy food. I was lonely and felt that I had no one to talk to.

The Lord whispered into my heart and gently showed me all the things that I did have. I had a roof over my head. My twenty-one-year-old car was parked in my garage, which is a fancier "house" than most of the world's humans live in. I was clothed, and I had a warm winter coat. I was healthy – not in the hospital, not hooked up to machines, not in a wheelchair. I had a job! And I had Him to talk to and confide in.

This point cannot be stressed enough. Give thanks to God for what you have, every day. If you thank Him daily, He will add more to you.

But rather seek ye the kingdom of God; and all these things shall be added unto you. (Luke 12:31)

And, I would like to add, if you complain about what you don't have, or about your circumstances, He will take more away from you, and your circumstances will become worse!

Warning number four: Are you bitter? Guess what – complaining always leads to bitterness. This is an extremely serious problem. Bitterness to the soul is like cancer to the body.

Looking diligently lest any man fail of the grace of God; lest any root of bitterness springing up trouble you, and thereby many be defiled. (Hebrews 12:15)

This is another power-packed verse that could be expounded upon for hours.

- Looking diligently: Examine your heart! Take stock of yourself every day, or every hour, if necessary. Is bitterness starting to grow in you?

I ran into a mother and son in the grocery store. This family used to attend my church. I asked them how they were doing. The teenaged son immediately started talking about the church and the church leaders. Almost every word he spoke was filled with bitterness. I was appalled that someone so young could be so bitter. We usually tend to think of a bitter old person, not a bitter teenager! I finally interrupted him and told him that if he really felt that way, it was his duty to pray for the people he was talking about (James 5:20). He replied, "Well, my parents already tried that, and it didn't work."

My heart was so grieved for this young man. What seeds of bitterness have been planted in his heart? Prayer always works! There is never a time when it doesn't. Just ask the woman who prayed for her mother for thirty-five years.

- Lest any man fail of the grace of God: We need God's grace to avoid bitterness!

We fail (receiving) the grace of God when we don't ask for it. God's grace is right there, readily available for you and me to reach out and take. When you feel bitterness creeping in, stop whatever you are doing or thinking, and ask God to remove it from your heart. He can and He will.

- Lest any root of bitterness springing up trouble you: Are you troubled by bitterness? Do you know someone who is?

I knew someone who always looked on the negative side of everything. I teased him once about winning the lottery. He replied (bitterly) that if he ever won the lottery, he would be stuck with paying taxes on all that money.

Really? If I (or most people) won the lottery, paying taxes would be the last thing on our minds.

I do not encourage buying lottery tickets. I am simply using this as an example of how bitterness can turn even an unexpected shower of money into a negative event.

- Bitterness defiles many! If you are bitter, everyone around you will be poisoned by your words and actions, and they will become bitter as well.

I have seen this happen too many times. Bitterness is like a virus that spreads from one infected person to another. Pretty soon the whole family, office, school or church is infected with bitterness.

Bitterness can be turned on its ear if you change your perspective. There is an old saying that you become what you look at. Instead of looking at your problems, look at Jesus. Amen!

Chapter 5: An unyielded heart

For the purposes of this book, I would like to put forth several synonyms for "cold." They are:

- Proud
- Stiff-necked
- Stubborn
- Unyielding
- Inflexible

These heart conditions are all tied together, and one leads to another.

I have learned, or at least I hope I have learned, to never say never. As soon as a person says "never," the Holy Spirit comes along and says, "Oh, yeah?"

For example:

- I can't ask her for help, because she was rude to me last year (or ten years ago, or when we were in kindergarten together, etc.), and she'll just be rude again if I ask.

- I'll never help that person again, because the last time I did, he didn't even say "thank you."

- I'll never go to that place again; I was so embarrassed by what happened when I was there before.

- I'm not going to apply for a job there again; they've turned me down too many times already.

Sure enough, you will find yourself with a flat tire by the side of the road, and the person you said you would "never" ask for help is the only one who stops to help you. Or, you will be the person driving by the guy stuck by the side of the road – the guy you said you would "never" help again, and no one else is stopping. Or, you need a job, and the only place that's hiring is the place you said you'd "never" apply to.

I was inwardly laughing at someone who told me she only uses sea salt. I thought, "I'll never buy sea salt; it's too expensive. Salt is salt – what's the big deal?" Then I found out all the chemicals that are artificially added to regular salt, and guess what? Now I only buy sea salt!

You can see an unyielded heart is evident in so many areas of people's lives:

- People will only vote for a candidate from a particular political party, because they have spent their lives telling everyone else how rotten the other parties are, so when a good candidate comes along from the "wrong" party, they won't vote for him/her. (What will people say? I can't vote for that person from the Rotten Party!)
- Someone will remain silent and watch his marriage crumble, rather than ask for forgiveness from his mate. (After all, it's the other person's fault; why should I have to say "I'm sorry?")
- Another person will find himself in an impossible situation, with every possible thing in his life going wrong, all because he made a wrong choice somewhere in the past, and the way out of the situation is simply to say, "I made a mistake," but he will never say it, because that would mean admitting he was wrong.

God had to deal very harshly with Israel several times because of their stubbornness.

Now be ye not stiffnecked, as your fathers were, but yield yourselves unto the LORD, and enter into his sanctuary, which he hath sanctified forever: and serve the LORD your God, that the fierceness of his wrath may turn away from you. (2 Chronicles 30:8)

Ye stiffnecked and uncircumcised in heart and ears, ye do always resist the Holy Ghost: as your fathers did, so do ye. (Acts 7:51)

The reason why we sometimes refuse to do God's will is because we think we know better than He does. As ridiculous as that seems, that's what Adam and Eve did when they ate the fruit. But there is a secret every Christian should know:

Delight thyself also in the LORD: and he shall give thee the desires of thine heart. (Psalm 37:4)

The word translated "delight" here means soft and pliable. If we remain soft and pliable in the hands of God, He will form us into whatever He wants us to be, and as a bonus, He will then give us the desires of our heart!

Adam and Eve wanted more than what God had already given them. They had perfect health, perfect peace, perfect safety, perfect love, perfect unity, perfect companionship, and perfect everything else, but it wasn't enough. Satan promised them something more – he promised them that they would be like God if they ate the fruit. Of course that was a lie, but they believed it, and stubbornly insisted on having their own way. Not only did they not become like

27

God when they ate the fruit, they were removed from the perfect environment He had provided for them, and thrust into a world that was evil and very far from perfect.

God has had to teach me this lesson so many times! I hope I have finally learned it.

You will ruin your life if you allow stubbornness to dictate to you what you will and won't do. Listen to me: it's not worth it.

Chapter 6: Unforgiveness

For if ye forgive men their trespasses, your heavenly Father will also forgive you: But if ye forgive not men their trespasses, neither will your Father forgive your trespasses. (Matthew 6:14-15)

Are there any unforgiven people in heaven? Is there a "forgiven" section and an "unforgiven" section?

Of course, I am being facetious.

We have to ask God, every day, to give us the supernatural power to forgive those who have hurt us. It is not a human thing that is within human capability; it is a God thing.

Unforgiveness is a deadly business. According to the verse above, if you do not forgive, God will not forgive you.

Like every other sin, we try to justify unforgiveness. We think the other person doesn't deserve it, after what he/she did to us.

Did the people who crucified Jesus deserve forgiveness?

Then said Jesus, Father, forgive them; for they know not what they do. And they parted his raiment, and cast lots. (Luke 23:34)

I have seen astounding examples of forgiveness in my lifetime. I personally know a woman who forgave her brother for sexually molesting her when she was a child. I know a woman who forgave her husband for abandoning her and moving in with another woman. I know a man who forgave his wife for committing adultery. I don't think any of these people are "super Christians;" I believe that they are people who allowed the Holy Spirit to work in their hearts and provide supernatural forgiveness to them, which they in turn were able to extend to those who had wronged them.

Forgiveness is absolutely essential to prevent a cold heart from developing. If someone has a cold heart, you can be almost certain that there is unforgiveness lurking somewhere in the background.

Unforgiveness has its root in pride. By refusing to forgive, you and I are saying, in essence, that we are better than the person who hurt us. We are also saying that we are better than God.

Probably none of us would dare to say out loud, "I am better than God." But consider this:

If we confess our sins, he is faithful and just to forgive us our sins, and to cleanse us from all unrighteousness. (1 John 1:9)

If we refuse to forgive, we are holding others to a higher standard than God holds them. We are elevating ourselves to a position above God, saying that even though He may forgive, we will not.

Unforgiveness results in torment. In Matthew 18, we read about someone who had been forgiven a huge financial debt. The lord (his master or boss) told him he didn't have to pay it back. Then the man who had been forgiven that huge debt went and demanded a small amount of money from another man who owed it to him. When that man couldn't pay, he had him thrown in prison. But when his master heard what he had done:

And his lord was wroth, and delivered him to the tormentors, till he should pay all that was due unto him. So likewise shall my heavenly Father do also unto you, if ye from your hearts forgive not everyone his brother their trespasses. (Matthew 18:34-35)

It is very tormenting to hold unforgiveness in your heart. You think day and night about the person who wronged you. It's been compared to letting someone you hate live in your head, rent-free. And ironically, the person you won't forgive probably has no idea of how you feel. He has gone on with his life, while you live a life of torment, locked into a prison of unforgiveness.

Take heed to yourselves: If thy brother trespass against thee, rebuke him; and if he repent, forgive him. And if he trespass against thee seven times in a day, and seven times in a day turn again to thee, saying, I repent; thou shalt forgive him. (Luke 17:3-4)

But what if the person has never asked you for forgiveness? Once again, we have Jesus as our example.

Then said Jesus, Father, forgive them; for they know not what they do. (Luke 23:34a)

The people who crucified our Lord didn't ask Him to forgive them. They didn't even know that they had done anything wrong. It wasn't until Peter preached to them, many days later, that they realized that they needed forgiveness.

Therefore let all the house of Israel know assuredly, that God hath made the same Jesus, whom ye have crucified, both Lord and Christ. Now when they heard this, they were pricked in their heart, and said unto Peter and to the rest of

31

the apostles, Men and brethren, what shall we do? Then Peter said unto them, Repent, and be baptized every one of you in the name of Jesus Christ for the remission of sins, and ye shall receive the gift of the Holy Ghost. (Acts 2:36-38)

Isn't it interesting that you cannot receive the Holy Spirit if you have not repented and asked for forgiveness? The person who wronged you needs to repent, certainly, but you and I also need to repent of our failure to forgive.

And when ye stand praying, forgive, if ye have ought against any: that your Father also which is in heaven may forgive you your trespasses. But if ye do not forgive, neither will your Father which is in heaven forgive your trespasses. (Mark 11:25-26)

All of the prayers in the world will not help you and me if we are holding unforgiveness in our hearts. Our prayers will just bounce off the ceiling and fall back and land on our own heads, more often than not resulting in a concussion!

Judge not, and ye shall not be judged: condemn not, and ye shall not be condemned: forgive, and ye shall be forgiven. (Luke 6:37)

I don't know about you, but I need forgiveness. Adam and Eve needed forgiveness, but the Bible doesn't record that they ever asked for it. If they had, the Lord would have forgiven them, and the world would not be in the state it is in today.

Chapter 7: Pride

What if you have asked someone to forgive you, and that person refuses? It means pride has taken hold in his heart.

One sin leads to another. Hiding from God leads to a failure to pray. Failing to pray leads to complaining. Complaining leads to bitterness. Bitterness leads to unforgiveness. Unforgiveness is caused by pride, and leads to more pride.

Pride is what made Heilel (mistranslated in our Bibles as Lucifer) become Satan. We are never more like Satan than when we are acting in pride.

The wicked, through the pride of his countenance, will not seek after God: God is not in all his thoughts. (Psalm 10:4)

I am thankful that the Lord loves me enough to knock me down to size whenever pride starts creeping in. Oh, my goodness – if I were to take an honest look at myself, I would see that there is nothing to be proud of.

For I know that in me (that is, in my flesh,) dwelleth no good thing: for to will is present with me; but how to perform that which is good I find not. (Romans 7:18)

If someone refuses to let you off the hook for something you have done, even though you have sincerely asked for forgiveness, do yourself a favor and let yourself off the hook. There comes a point when you have done all you can humanly do. Release yourself from the other person's unforgiveness, and go in peace. Remember, he or she is living in torment. There is no reason for you to live there, too.

Therefore pride compasseth them about as a chain; violence covereth them as a garment. (Psalm 73:6)

What if you are the one with pride in your heart?

I once knew someone who was so prideful, she was proud of being proud! Looking behind the façade of her pride, I saw someone who was terribly insecure and frightened of being exposed. It was a sad situation, because everyone who knew this person could see right through her. People who are insecure talk the most and the loudest, push their way to the front of every line, love giving orders to everyone else, and will *never* admit it when they are wrong. This person caused a lot of destruction and division in our church. When she was finally confronted, she left the church, rather than admit wrongdoing and ask for forgiveness. She left thinking that no one knew what was going on, and yet everyone knew; it was obvious.

Such a person reminds me of a cat I used to have. Annie would hide under the bed, thinking I couldn't see her. Trouble was, her tail was always sticking out. I would play a little game with her. I would stand next to the bed and call, "Annie, where are you?" She would remain motionless under the bed, with her tail sticking out in full view. I would then reach down and tweak her tail. This always caused her to jump! But she never figured out that when she was "hiding" from me, I knew exactly where she was.

Adam and Eve hid behind the trees, saying to themselves, "God will never find us here. He can't see us."

Oh, little man! What foolish pride causes you to think that God doesn't see you?

If someone asks you to forgive him, please forgive him immediately. Please don't wait until you feel like forgiving. That feeling may never come. Feelings follow actions. If you forgive, asking God to help you, eventually you will feel in your heart that you have truly forgiven. You will feel a lightness and a joy that you didn't have before.

If you have sincerely asked another person for forgiveness, and been rebuffed, forgive the other person for not forgiving you! Then go in peace.

Forgiveness is a pride-killer. No one deserves forgiveness, but we all need it.

Chapter 8: Weeds

And the LORD God took the man, and put him into the garden of Eden to dress it and to keep it. (Genesis 2:15)

This verse always fascinated me. Dress it? Keep it?

Dressing involves tending, working, cultivating. Keeping involves guarding. Before the fall, Adam's job was to take care of the garden. But, I thought the garden was a perfect place. Why would a perfect place need work?

I confess I don't fully know the answer. I do know that work, like everything else, was very different before and after the fall.

God worked when he created the universe. It took him six days, and on the seventh day he rested from His work. That simply means he stopped what He was doing.

Thus the heavens and the earth were finished, and all the host of them. And on the seventh day God ended his work which he had made; and he rested on the seventh day from all his work which he had made. And God blessed the seventh day, and sanctified it: because that in it he had rested from all his work which God created and made. (Genesis 2:1-3)

I don't think God got tired from creating the universe. I don't think He needed to sleep afterwards. I believe the act of creation brought great joy to Him.

And God saw everything that he had made, and, behold, it was very good. (Genesis 1:31a)

We get tiny glimpses of this as human beings. God has placed within each one of us tremendous creative potential. Why? Because He created us to be like Him.

And God said, Let us make man in our image, after our likeness... (Genesis 1:26a)

Look at the potential that is within you! God created you to do so many different things. People make handcrafted furniture and handmade quilts, rebuild car engines from scratch, build houses and bridges from the ground up, make delicious desserts and beautiful jewelry, and paint breathtaking paintings. Doctors put back together broken bodies and re-build broken bones and teeth. A woman carries a child in her womb for nine months and then delivers a tiny miracle.

And gardeners plant flowers, vegetables, shrubbery and trees, water them, prune them, and get rid of all the weeds.

Whenever you or I create something, we are living out the creative potential that God placed within us. We look at the things that we have made, and they give us joy.

I believe Adam's job in taking care of the garden was intended to give him joy. Who knows, maybe he told the lemon trees to move over to the south side on Monday, then told the date palms to grow into the shape of a circle on Tuesday. Whatever work he did, it was satisfying and rewarding.

After the fall, the nature of work changed.

...cursed is the ground for thy sake; in sorrow shalt thou eat of it all the days of thy life; thorns also and thistles shall it bring forth to thee; and thou shalt eat the herb of

the field; in the sweat of thy face shalt thou eat bread, till thou return unto the ground; for out of it wast thou taken: for dust thou art, and unto dust shalt thou return. (Genesis 3:17b-19)

After the fall, Adam's work involved sweat and labor. At the end of each day, he was worn out from working, and needed to sleep. His muscles hurt, and he probably had a headache. Work wasn't fun anymore; it was just work.

God shows me so much when I am working in my yard. It is my own tiny little piece of Eden, and I treasure it. Every spring I plant flowers, move the birdbath around, find a new place to hang the wind chimes, etc., and I have a blast doing it. But it's work! I can't sit at my kitchen table and look out my patio door, and simply will the flowers to be planted and grow, and the flower pots to be placed where I want them. I have to do it myself, by the sweat of my face, and believe me, it is sweaty work.

And the weeds! God spoke to me while I was pulling weeds. I couldn't understand how I could pull weeds, day after day, and yet always find new weeds growing the next day. Where do all these weeds come from, anyway?

Thorns also and thistles shall it bring forth to thee…

Here is what God showed me. The weeds in my garden are like every rotten thing in my heart. I can identify each thing that is not pleasing to Him, repent of it, and ask Him to remove it. And He does. The next day, I need to repeat the process. And the day after that, I need to repeat it again.

Another fitting analogy is showering. I take a shower on Saturday, and on Sunday, I need another shower.

What if you or I pulled all the weeds out of our gardens, then took a shower and sat down and said, "Thank goodness that's done. I'll never have to pull weeds or take a shower again." In a very short time, our gardens would become impassable jungles, and no one would come within a ten-foot radius of us!

Too many Christians receive salvation on a certain day, and believe they are now complete. No, the work has just begun.

Chapter 9: Leaves

Leaves are pretty, but they are not fruit.

A tree covered with leaves in the spring and summer makes a delightful place to rest in the shade. But if you are hungry, you can't eat leaves. You need fruit.

Many people have "leaves" – in other words, they look good on the outside to others. But they have nothing to offer anyone who is spiritually hungry, and nothing to show that God is working in their hearts.

There are many Christian denominations today. They all have one thing in common. At the time of their founding, they had received a portion of the truth from God, and they took that truth and made it the founding principle of their denomination, and stopped there. They had beautiful leaves, and some of them even had some fruit, but because they did not go any further with God, whatever fruit they may have had died, and they were left with leaves. They look good on the outside.

Have you ever wondered why we have eternity? It's because we are designed to never stop growing or learning. I need eternity to understand God and become like Him.

I wish I could explain this truth to all the denominations. "You have the Bible? Good; there's more. You have salvation? Good; there's more. You have the Holy Spirit? Good; there's more. You send missionaries all over the world? Good; there's more. You preach the gospel every day? Good; there's more. You have miracles? Good; there's more. You have all the spiritual gifts listed in the Bible? Good; there's more. You have overcome the world, the flesh, and the devil? Good; there's more."

People are limited as to what they can receive from God, only by their willingness to receive it. If I had ten thousand years here on this earth, in this body, to study the Bible, I would still be only scratching the surface of its truths. That's why I need eternity.

The Christian life is not easy. We all get tired. When we are tired, we are tempted to stop where we are, with only our leaves, and say that we have arrived. But I believe there were an infinite variety of trees in Eden, bearing infinite varieties of fruit, and like them, I want to continue to grow, learn, expand, and produce. God help me, if I ever stop, I hope He takes me home.

Chapter 10: Don't be offended

And blessed is he, whosoever shall not be offended in me. (Matthew 11:6)

Jesus spoke those words to the disciples of John the Baptist. John was in prison, and he was starting to doubt. John was the one who baptized Jesus in the Jordan river – the one who spoke these words about Him:

Behold the Lamb of God, which taketh away the sin of the world. This is he of whom I said, After me cometh a man which is preferred before me: for he was before me. And I knew him not: but that he should be made manifest to Israel, therefore am I come baptizing with water. And John bare record, saying, I saw the Spirit descending from heaven like a dove, and it abode upon him. And I knew him not: but he that sent me to baptize with water, the same said unto me, Upon whom thou shalt see the Spirit descending, and remaining on him, the same is he which baptizeth with the Holy Ghost. And I saw, and bare record that this is the Son of God. (John 1:29b-34)

Jesus told John's disciples to go back to John in prison and tell him not to be offended in Jesus (Matthew 11:6). This is a verse I had read all my life, and never understood until the Holy Spirit revealed its meaning to me.

John knew that Jesus of Nazareth was the Messiah. John spent his life preparing the way for Jesus. John said, "This is the Son of God."

But then, John was thrown into prison. In his dark prison cell, he began to doubt.

Have you ever doubted?

It breaks my heart when I think about various people I have known over the years, who started out strong on their journey with Jesus, and ended up leaving Him by the side of the road. Why? Because they became offended in Jesus.

Being offended in Jesus is different than being offended by Jesus. I suppose the Pharisees were offended by Jesus when he called them a generation of snakes.

Ye serpents, ye generation of vipers, how can ye escape the damnation of hell? (Matthew 23:33).

But being offended in Jesus means being offended by what He is asking you to do, or being offended by the troubles that have come into your life while serving Him.

John loved Jesus, and dedicated his life to proclaiming that He was the Messiah. But his life didn't turn out the way he thought it would. My life hasn't, and I'll bet yours hasn't, either.

It's when we are in prison – whether an actual prison, or the prison of our own disappointments – that we begin to doubt Him. And if we're not careful, we will become offended.

John the Baptist, by all accounts, was a bit of an oddball. He lived in the desert, ate insects, wore strange clothing, and probably didn't bathe very often. The Bible doesn't tell us when the Holy Spirit spoke to John and told him that he would see the Spirit descending on Jesus. But He did speak to him, and John believed what he heard. I think John thought, as so many of us do, that if he obeyed the directions of the Holy Spirit, his life would be smooth sailing. I'm sure that John never dreamed he would end up in prison.

This is the heart of the matter.

When we set out to do God's will, very often our lives become worse, not better. Scripture is full of examples of this. Abel obeyed the Lord and gave Him a sacrifice that pleased Him, and was murdered as a result (Genesis 4:4-8). Elijah obeyed the Lord and had a tremendous victory when he defeated the false prophets of Baal, but less than twenty-four hours later he was running for his life and was suicidal (1 Kings 18 & 19). David was anointed as king of Israel, but didn't take the throne until about thirteen years later, and those years were spent running and hiding from Saul, who wanted to kill him (1 Samuel 16:13, 1 Samuel 18-27, 2 Samuel 5:4).

It is easy to become offended in Jesus. When we are offended in Him, our hearts become cold. It is absolutely essential that we don't allow this to happen.

Chapter 11: False salvation

I believe the reason why so many people become offended in Jesus is because of the way salvation has been watered down and misrepresented in the church today. As an illustration of this, I was talking to a young man who was a member of a mainline denomination. I mentioned the phrase "born again." He responded by saying that he was born again when he was baptized by being sprinkled with water when he was an infant.

I haven't found that idea in the scriptures, but that's very typical of the mainline church experience. But in the evangelical church, it's just as bad.

Salvation is stressed as a requirement for entering heaven. But salvation is presented as something that happens to a person once, on a fixed day and time. This watered-down salvation is the cause of much disappointment and apostasy in the church today.

I remember being seven years old, and hearing the gospel (or a form of it) being presented at church. I remember hearing the description of hell as being a place of unending torment and separation from God. In my seven-year-old mind I thought, "That sounds terrible! I never want to go there!" So, when the invitation to receive Christ came, I walked down the aisle and received "salvation."

But what is salvation? What is it really?

I can tell you that salvation is a continuous process. No doubt many people will be offended by that statement, but it is true.

- Salvation *comes* from God. It is a free gift. No human being has ever saved himself, nor ever will.
- Salvation *begins* when the individual recognizes that he is a sinner and he needs forgiveness.
- Salvation *grows* when the person sincerely asks God to forgive him of his sins.
- Salvation *continues* as the person turns away from his sin. This is a one hundred and eighty-degree turn. He goes the opposite way of the way he was going before.
- Salvation *remains* as the person lives a life of daily repentance and turning to God.
- Salvation is *preserved* as the individual refuses to be offended in Jesus!

The salvation I received at the age of seven was the forgiveness of my sins, when I realized that I was a sinner. I wonder how much different my life would have been if the gospel had been presented to me this way:

"You are a sinner and you need God to forgive you. Ask Him to forgive you. Then, dedicate your life to Him. When you do that, you will be mocked, misunderstood, laughed at, and cursed at. The people that you thought were your friends will walk away from you. Family members will walk away from you. You will lose your (so-called) good reputation. You will probably become financially impoverished. You will be very lonely. God will ask you to do things that you are absolutely unable to do. You will no longer feel comfortable here on this earth, because you will be longing for heaven. You will feel like a fish out of water. Now, whoever wants to receive Jesus as his savior, please come forward."

Would I have come forward? Would you?

Please don't misunderstand. I am grateful that Jesus forgave me of my sins. But I look back at my life and see the many times I became offended in Jesus. He would ask me to do something, and I would start out to do it with good intentions, but in a short time find opposition and obstacles. According to the diluted gospel I had believed, if you're doing God's will, that will not happen to you. So, I would abandon whatever it was I had set out to do, and complain to God about it. And my heart would get a little bit colder each time.

For a great door and effectual is opened unto me, and there are many adversaries. (1 Corinthians 16:9)

Satan opposes God and His people. When God opens a door for you, you can be certain that Satan is right there, trying to prevent you from walking through it, or trying to slam it in your face.

I read an article about a well-known preacher and author who left the faith. He made the statement, "I no longer consider myself a Christian." I would be willing to bet money that this man at one point in his life received the standard partial gospel that is so prevalent today. He made a "decision" for Christ, and when things didn't go the way he planned, he became offended and walked away.

Bitterness defiles many! Today, when people have "followers" on social media, people follow others blindly without looking where they are going, even if they are going off a cliff! This man fell and took many of his followers with him. It's one thing to walk away from God yourself, but walking away never ends with just you.

But whoso shall offend one of these little ones which believe in me, it were better for him that a millstone were hanged about his neck, and that he were drowned in the depth of the sea. (Matthew 18:6)

Satan wants to destroy your faith. He wants to take you down and take as many others with you as he can. Don't let him!

The thief cometh not, but for to steal, and to kill, and to destroy: I am come that they might have life, and that they might have it more abundantly. (John 10:10)

Many churches are focused on expanding their congregations. In the evangelical church, this is accomplished by presenting the (first part of the) gospel and inviting people to come forward and make a decision for Christ. Rarely, if ever, are people told the truth about what it really means to be a Christian and to follow Him.

I am here to tell you the truth. If you decide to truly follow Jesus Christ, you will follow Him all the way to the cross. The cross is a place of execution. No one wants to be executed, but for the Christian, it is a necessity. It's very unlikely that your physical body will be nailed to a physical cross, but if you are His disciple, your hopes, dreams, human plans and aspirations, even if they are good and beautiful, will be put to death on His cross.

And they that are Christ's have crucified the flesh with the affections and lusts. (Galatians 5:24)

That is genuine salvation, and there is no other way.

Chapter 12: Laziness

Everything in the Christian life is hard work. After receiving salvation, which is free and easy, the work begins.

Let's be honest. Many of us don't like to work. We would prefer for life to be easy, all the time. But it's not. Life is hard for the unbeliever, and life is hard for the believer. The difference is, the believer has a helper: the Holy Spirit.

Nevertheless I tell you the truth; It is expedient for you that I go away: for if I go not away, the Comforter will not come unto you; but if I depart, I will send him unto you. (John 16:7)

Jesus spoke these words to His disciples, right before He was crucified. Like most of what He told them, they didn't fully understand.

Without the Holy Spirit, life is unbearable for you and me. But with Him, all things are possible.

And Jesus looking upon them saith, With men it is impossible, but not with God: for with God all things are possible. (Mark 10:27)

The Lord has asked me to do things that are humanly impossible. I have told Him (as if He didn't already know), "Lord, this is impossible. I can't do this." Then, I have seen with my own eyes the hand of God working in my life and others' lives in a way that defies explanation. How? Because it is the Holy Spirit working in me, doing through me what I am unable to do on my own.

One of my favorite quotes is attributed to Mother Teresa: "I belong to Jesus Christ. He must be allowed to use me, as He wishes, without consulting me."

We all have a tendency to put the cart before the horse. Instead of saying, "I can't do this; it's too hard," we need to say, "God, You can do anything. Nothing is too hard for You. If You want me to do this, just work through me and use me." When faced with an impossible task, ask Him to take over. He will.

Our flesh wins the battle too many times. Pulling weeds (removing the ungodly things from our hearts) is hard work. Forgiveness is hard work. Uprooting pride is hard work. Bearing fruit is hard work.

We've all seen neglected yards and gardens. Sometimes it's downright painful to look at them. I've seen gardens with beautiful flowers that are almost choked out by weeds, because no one has taken the time to pull them. The potential for beauty is there, but laziness prevented it from happening. Eden was perfect – no weeds, no fruit-eating pests, yet Adam still had to tend it. In order to produce beauty, work is required.

Through a series of painful circumstances, I began to look at my life as belonging to Jesus, not myself. I was forced to lay aside a lot of things, very good things, that I wanted for myself, and exchange them for His cross.

Carrying a cross is hard work.

And he said to them all, If any man will come after me, let him deny himself, and take up his cross daily, and follow me. (Luke 9:23)

I have learned the hard way that I need to begin every day's work with prayer. Before I get out of bed, I ask the Lord to help me pick up my cross. I ask Him to give me the strength to carry it. I ask Him to put joy in my heart as I'm doing what He has called me to do.

Therefore, my beloved brethren, be ye stedfast, unmoveable, always abounding in the work of the Lord, forasmuch as ye know that your labour is not in vain in the Lord. (1 Corinthians 15:58)

Laziness prevents you and me from reaching our full potential in Jesus Christ. A potential Olympic athlete will never reach the Olympic games by sitting on the couch, eating potato chips. Likewise, you and I will never reach the finish line in the race that is set before us (Hebrews 12:1) if we don't continue running.

What has God told you to do? Whatever it is, do not waver from it. If it is impossible to do, do it anyway, one day, one hour, one minute at a time. Our flesh is so lazy! We don't want to do what God has asked of us, because honestly, it's easier not to. I mean, it is easier in the natural realm. But you and I usually don't see what the end result of our obedience to Him will be when we start out. We just need to obey, and let Him take care of the rest.

Chapter 13: Listening to the Holy Spirit

It is very sad that many prominent preachers today say that God no longer speaks. They teach that He spoke through His word (the Bible) long ago, and has been silent ever since.

I shudder to think that where I go to school, who I marry, what job I take, and where I live, are all up to me. Left to myself, I will make the wrong choice every time. All of these questions are of great importance and have huge consequences, and none of their answers will be found in the Bible. Please don't be like the person who needed guidance from God, so he shut his eyes, opened the Bible at random, and jabbed his finger down on a page, then opened his eyes and read, "...and (Judas) went and hanged himself." He then closed his eyes again, opened the Bible at random again, jabbed his finger down on another page, and read, "Go, and do thou likewise."

It is very true that God still speaks to us in a still, small voice.

And after the earthquake a fire; but the LORD was not in the fire: and after the fire a still small voice. (1 Kings 19:12).

If you are disappointed, hurt, angry and upset that something in your life didn't go as you had planned, you may not want to hear anything further from God. You may shut your ears and turn away from Him, then make excuses as to why you can't (won't) obey Him. This will cause your heart to grow cold.

And the LORD God called unto Adam, and said unto him, Where art thou? And he said, I heard thy voice in the garden, and I was afraid, because I was naked; and I hid myself. And he said, Who told thee that thou wast naked? Hast thou eaten of the tree, whereof I commanded thee that thou shouldest not eat? And the man said, The woman whom thou gavest to be with me, she gave me of the tree, and I did eat. (Genesis 3:9-12)

It truly makes me want to cry when I read about the fall of man. It has been said that Eve was deceived – in other words, she honestly believed that eating the fruit was the right thing to do. But it's also been said that Adam deliberately sinned. He *knew* he shouldn't eat the fruit, but he did it anyway.

Don't disregard God's voice.

"But how do I know when God is speaking to me?" someone will ask. Good question! Here are some answers:

- You will have a thought that stays with you night and day.

For seven years (yes, seven), I felt a very strong impression that I needed to paint a particular painting. I saw it clearly in my mind's eye. It seemed like too big of a project for me to undertake. In school, I had enjoyed art class, and painted a few little things here and there. But this painting was *big*. I don't mean its physical size. I'm talking about the message that it was to convey. It seemed far beyond my capabilities.

Finally, I obeyed. The painting took a long time. When it was finally finished, I stood back and looked at it, and I realized with great humiliation that the painting had nothing to do with me or my so-called skills or abilities. It was something that God Himself had painted. He just

53

happened to use my hand to do it. I repented for the next seven years, for not acting quickly when I first felt the impression to paint it. I firmly believe that if I had flat-out refused in my spirit to paint it, the impression would have eventually left me. I would have lost the blessing that God wanted to give me, and others would have missed out on a blessing as well.

That painting is now hanging on the wall of my church. I thank God that He never let the thought leave me, despite my foolishness and wasting so much time.

- You will have a thought or impression that comes out of the blue.

If you are thinking about your kitchen and what color you should paint it, and the thought comes to you: "Yellow," I'm pretty sure that is just one of the many thoughts you have every day. (Note: If you are "thinking" about what color to paint your kitchen, not "praying" about it, your own thoughts will tell you what color to paint it. But if you're praying about it, the Holy Spirit will tell you! He cares about everything we pray about, big or small, even our kitchens.)

But, if you are thinking about your kitchen and what color you should paint it, and you have a thought such as, "Pray for Susan," you need to drop everything and pray for Susan. Susan has nothing to do with your kitchen's colors, but everything to do with God's plan.

This is illustrated perfectly by a sobering true story. The pastor of my church was watching a preacher on TV one night. He was thinking about nothing other than what he was seeing on the screen. Without warning, his mind was suddenly flooded with the image of a woman he knew.

54

With it came the certain realization that she was in trouble. He immediately began praying for her. He knew nothing of her situation – he knew nothing at all, he just prayed for her for about half an hour, until the feeling lifted, and he felt peace in his heart. Much later he found out that at the exact moment he had felt the overwhelming urge to pray for her, she had been in terrible danger in a stranger's hotel room, about to be raped. She had managed to lock herself in the bathroom and call 911, and the police rescued her from that situation.

What would have happened if he hadn't prayed for her? What if he would have said, "I want to watch this TV program; I'll pray for her later?"

Don't ignore God's voice.

- The thought or impression that you have will always align with the Bible. If it doesn't, it's not from God.

Yes, some people have some very weird thoughts and attribute them to God. We all know this. The thought that you are having that tells you to divorce your wife, help yourself to your neighbor's belongings, or lie on your resume in order to get that great job, is not from God. This should be so obvious, but it is amazing how many Christians talk themselves into situations because they "heard the voice of God."

Satan is a master at masquerading as God! The Bible says he appears as an angel of light.

And no marvel; for Satan himself is transformed into an angel of light (2 Corinthians 11:14).

And, after he convinces someone to act, he then immediately accuses that person of the sin he/she just committed.

And I heard a loud voice saying in heaven, Now is come salvation, and strength, and the kingdom of our God, and the power of his Christ: for the accuser of our brethren is cast down, which accused them before our God day and night (Revelation 12:10).

Make sure your thoughts align with God's word.

- God will not always tell you pleasant things.

Wouldn't it be nice if He did? But He doesn't.

Years ago I had an issue with a coworker. This person had treated me very unfairly. I was angry and resentful about what had happened, so I dealt with the situation by talking about her behind her back. The Holy Spirit began gently nudging me to apologize to her for gossiping about her. To say that I didn't want to do this is a massive understatement! But He kept impressing this upon me. Finally, I made up my mind to do it. I wanted to wait until I was sure I could speak to her in private, with no one overhearing our conversation. It's very strange that the thing I absolutely did not want to do became something I couldn't wait to do, once I finally made the decision to do it. So, when I knew we could be alone, I apologized and asked her to forgive me. The shock on her face was evident.

This was a soul- and flesh-crushing experience. I knew for a fact that I never, never wanted to ever, ever have to do that ever, ever again, and the only way to not have to do it again was to stop gossiping about her. It was a humiliating lesson to have to learn, and I'm so glad He loved me enough to teach it to me.

This could have turned out very differently. When God spoke to me, I could have justified my actions by saying that she deserved to have people talking about her behind her back, and that she should be the one to apologize to me.

Adam tried to justify his actions by blaming Eve.

If we stubbornly refuse to obey His voice, He will eventually stop speaking to us. Oh, how cold the human heart is that doesn't hear from God.

Don't ignore His voice.

Chapter 14: Ignoring other voices

Now the serpent was more subtil than any beast of the field which the LORD God had made. And he said unto the woman, Yea, hath God said, Ye shall not eat of every tree of the garden? (Genesis 3:1)

The instruction that God gave to Adam was so clear: don't eat the fruit from the tree of the knowledge of good and evil. But when Eve listened to another voice (Satan's) it brought confusion to her. She began to doubt what God had said. When Adam listened to another voice (Eve's), he also became confused. They both ended up disobeying God's voice and following another voice.

The Bible is full of examples of this.

And Ahab told Jezebel all that Elijah had done, and withal how he had slain all the prophets with the sword. Then Jezebel sent a messenger unto Elijah, saying, So let the gods do to me, and more also, if I make not thy life as the life of one of them by tomorrow about this time. (1 Kings 19:1-2)

Elijah had just had a tremendous victory. He had just killed four hundred and fifty prophets of Baal. Jezebel was enraged when she heard this. She vowed to kill Elijah. What did Elijah do? He listened to her voice and ran away.

And when he saw that, he arose, and went for his life, and came to Beersheba, which belongeth to Judah, and left his servant there. But he himself went a day's journey into the wilderness, and came and sat down under a juniper tree: and he requested for himself that he might die; and said, It is enough; now, O LORD, take away my life; for I am not better than my fathers. (1 Kings 19:3-4)

God was very merciful to Elijah. Even though he ran away, God still sent an angel that brought him food and water, and enabled him to travel on to the next town. God rebuked Elijah and reminded him that he was not the only prophet of God.

When we read the full account of how Elijah called fire down from heaven to burn up the sacrifice, then killed the false prophets, it's hard to understand how he could listen to the threats of Jezebel and run away.

In 1 Kings 13 we read about a young prophet who was told to go and give a word to king Jeroboam. The Lord gave him very specific instructions about not eating or drinking in the city he was sent to. He was told to give the word and get out. But another, older prophet heard about what the young prophet had done, and he was jealous. As the young man was leaving town, the older man went after him.

Then he said unto him, Come home with me, and eat bread. And he said, I may not return with thee, nor go in with thee: neither will I eat bread nor drink water with thee in this place: For it was said to me by the word of the LORD, Thou shalt eat no bread nor drink water there, nor turn again to go by the way that thou camest. He said unto him, I am a prophet also as thou art; and an angel spake unto me by the word of the LORD, saying, Bring him back with thee into thine house, that he may eat bread and drink water. But he lied unto him. So he went back with him, and did eat bread in his house, and drank water. (1 Kings 13:15-19)

The young prophet listened to the old prophet's voice, disobeying what God had already told him to do, and lost his life. A lion killed him on his way home.

God spoke to Abram and told him that he would have a son. Abram believed the promise of God, but it was a long time coming.

And Abram said, Behold, to me thou hast given no seed: and, lo, one born in my house is mine heir. And, behold, the word of the LORD came unto him, saying, This shall not be thine heir; but he that shall come forth out of thine own bowels shall be thine heir. And he brought him forth abroad, and said, Look now toward heaven, and tell the stars, if thou be able to number them: and he said unto him, So shall thy seed be. And he believed in the LORD; and he counted it to him for righteousness. (Genesis 15:3-6)

Then Abram got tired of waiting.

Now Sarai Abram's wife bare him no children: and she had an handmaid, an Egyptian, whose name was Hagar. And Sarai said unto Abram, Behold now, the LORD hath restrained me from bearing: I pray thee, go in unto my maid; it may be that I may obtain children by her. And Abram hearkened to the voice of Sarai. And Sarai Abram's wife took Hagar her maid the Egyptian, after Abram had dwelt ten years in the land of Canaan, and gave her to her husband Abram to be his wife. And he went in unto Hagar, and she conceived: and when she saw that she had conceived, her mistress was despised in her eyes. (Genesis 16:1-4)

Elijah listened to a voice other than God's, and wasted a lot of time running away. The young prophet listened to another prophet's voice, ignoring God's instructions, and died as a result. Abram listened to his wife, forgot about what God had told him, and had a child by another woman.

These accounts are very sobering. Each one of these people had a word from God, but chose to listen to other people instead. It is a very serious thing to take the word of a human being over the word of God. It has disastrous consequences.

Once you or I get a word from God, we need to cling onto that word with all our might. Don't let go of it, no matter what anyone says. People who are older and wiser than you will come to you with lots of advice as to what you should do. If it contradicts what God has already told you, don't do it.

When Elijah was about to be taken by God, he kept telling his friend Elisha to stay behind.

And Elijah said unto Elisha, Tarry here, I pray thee; for the LORD hath sent me to Bethel. And Elisha said unto him, As the LORD liveth, and as thy soul liveth, I will not leave thee. So they went down to Bethel. And Elijah said unto him, Elisha, tarry here, I pray thee; for the LORD hath sent me to Jericho. And he said, As the LORD liveth, and as thy soul liveth, I will not leave thee. So they came to Jericho. And Elijah said unto him, Tarry, I pray thee, here; for the LORD hath sent me to Jordan. And he said, As the LORD liveth, and as thy soul liveth, I will not leave thee. And they two went on. (2 Kings 2:2, 4, 6)

I don't know why Elijah kept telling Elisha to stay behind. Perhaps he was testing him to see if he would obey the voice of his friend rather than the voice of God. Thankfully, Elisha passed the test. He stayed with Elijah until the Lord took Elijah away, and as a result, he got a double portion of Elijah's anointing.

You and I must learn to ignore other's voices. We should always try to be kind and respectful to those who have a different opinion, but in the final analysis, we will not stand before people on the day of judgment; we will stand before God.

So then every one of us shall give account of himself to God. (Romans 14:12)

I don't want to stand before God with a bunch of excuses. "Well God, You see, I know You told me to do this thing, but so-and-so told me I should do something else, so that's what I did." Like Adam and Eve hiding behind the trees, when I make excuses, I have nowhere to go. My position is indefensible.

It is a fearful thing to fall into the hands of the living God. (Hebrews 10:31)

On the other hand, we need to be very careful that we are not the person who is talking someone else out of what God has told him or her to do. Parents, especially, are guilty of this too often. If we see our child on a very hard path, we want to rescue him from the pain of that path, even when it is God's chosen path for him.

Let us not therefore judge one another anymore: but judge this rather, that no man put a stumblingblock or an occasion to fall in his brother's way. (Romans 14:13)

Let's get out of other people's way, and get out of our own way, and let God have His way. Amen.

Chapter 15: Not in the winter

But pray ye that your flight be not in the winter, neither on the sabbath day... (Matthew 24:20)

Like the verse in Genesis about walking with God in the cool of the day – a misunderstanding of what the scripture says – I have heard a lot of preachers warning about fleeing in the winter. When Jesus returns to earth, I guarantee that if it's summer in one geographical location, it will be winter in another.

(When it is winter in the United States, it is summer in Australia.)

Pray that your heart is not cold when Jesus returns! There are many warnings in the scripture about this.

Therefore be ye also ready: for in such an hour as ye think not the Son of man cometh. (Matthew 24:44)

But and if that evil servant shall say in his heart, My lord delayeth his coming; And shall begin to smite his fellowservants, and to eat and drink with the drunken; The lord of that servant shall come in a day when he looketh not for him, and in an hour that he is not aware of, And shall cut him asunder, and appoint him his portion with the hypocrites: there shall be weeping and gnashing of teeth. (Matthew 24:48-51)

Watch ye therefore: for ye know not when the master of the house cometh, at even, or at midnight, or at the cockcrowing, or in the morning: Lest coming suddenly he find you sleeping. And what I say unto you I say unto all, Watch. (Mark 13:35-37)

Jesus does not care if you are sleeping in your bed when He returns! Mark 13:36 is referring to your spiritual condition. When you are spiritually asleep, you are unaware of what is going on around you. Some people are merely asleep, and others are in cryogenic sleep!

As my mother always said, "Many are cold. A few are frozen."

When I read the writings of great believers who have gone on to be with the Lord, one thing strikes me about all of them. They all believed that He would return in their lifetime.

This is the attitude we should all have. No one knows the hour or the day when He is coming, but each one of us should live as if it is today, this afternoon, this evening. We should be expectant and ready for anything. The cold heart says, "Oh, well, it probably won't be for many more years. There's no reason to get excited over it."

Friends, Jesus cannot come soon enough to suit me. There is nothing in this world, or the systems or programs of this world, that has any appeal to me. I want to be like Him. I want to see Him as He is. I want Eden!

Do you?

Chapter 16: Keeping the garden

Eden symbolizes so many things. Of course, it is a real place, with a real garden, with real trees bearing real fruit. But it also is a spiritual place. Eden symbolizes the perfection of unity between God and man.

I mentioned weeds earlier. They keep springing up in our natural gardens. We can pull every weed out on Saturday, and on Sunday, new weeds have grown.

This is tending the garden. But God also told Adam to keep the garden.

And the LORD God took the man, and put him into the garden of Eden to dress it and to keep it. (Genesis 2:15)

What does keep mean? It means to guard.

Eve gets a lot of criticism for eating the forbidden fruit, and she should. But what about Adam?

Now the serpent was more subtil than any beast of the field which the LORD God had made. And he said unto the woman, Yea, hath God said, Ye shall not eat of every tree of the garden? (Genesis 3:1)

Question: What was Satan doing in the garden?

What happened? Did Adam knowingly let Satan into the garden? Was it an accident? Did Satan sneak into the garden?

It is disturbing to read the sequence of events as they are recorded in Genesis.

And God saw everything that he had made, and, behold, it was very good. (Genesis 1:31a)

And the LORD God took the man, and put him into the garden of Eden to dress it and to keep it. (Genesis 2:15)

And the LORD God said, It is not good that the man should be alone; I will make him an help meet for him. (Genesis 2:18)

Why did God say that everything was "very good," and then say later that it was "not good" for the man to be alone?

God warned Adam, before Eve was created, not to eat fruit from the tree of the knowledge of good and evil.

But of the tree of the knowledge of good and evil, thou shalt not eat of it: for in the day that thou eatest thereof thou shalt surely die. (Genesis 2:17)

The Bible doesn't record that God ever gave Eve this warning. We can infer that it was Adam's job to pass the warning on to Eve.

Did he?

I am of the opinion that sometime before Eve was created, Adam let Satan into the garden. Either he was sleeping on the job that God gave him to do (figuratively if not literally), or he deliberately did it. Either way, the situation that God had pronounced to be "very good" suddenly became "not good."

We need to think very carefully about the words that God used. "It is not good that the man should be alone..." Of all people who ever lived, Adam was not alone! Adam had perfect unity with God before the fall. Adam was not separated from God because of sin, as you and I are without Christ. Adam talked with God one on one. Adam understood God and had an intimate fellowship with Him that no one else has ever had, except Jesus Christ.

In the New Testament, we read about how the Sadducees tried to trick Jesus into saying something that went against the Jewish law. They told him a story about a man who died, having no children, and the man's brother married his dead brother's widow and had no children, and all seven of the brothers in that family ended up marrying her and leaving no children. They asked Jesus:

Therefore, in the resurrection whose wife shall she be of the seven? For they all had her. Jesus answered and said unto them, Ye do err, not knowing the scriptures, nor the power of God. For in the resurrection they neither marry, nor are given in marriage, but are as the angels of God in heaven. (Matthew 22:28-30)

I believe that Adam, living in a sinless body in a sinless environment, was also like the angels of God in heaven, in the sense that his fellowship with Him was so perfect, he needed nothing else.

And the LORD God said, It is not good that the man should be alone; I will make him an help meet for him. (Genesis 2:18)

Once again, I cannot be dogmatic about this, but it seems to me that God saw that Adam needed a suitable helper after the snake got into the garden. Perhaps He saw that Adam's heart was beginning to grow cold toward God, and that coldness was what made an opening for Satan to enter the garden. I believe it was Eve's job to encourage Adam to listen to and obey the voice of God. And, perhaps she did, for a time. We don't know how long after God created her that the fall occurred.

So, Adam failed by not keeping the garden, and Eve failed by not helping her husband obey what God had commanded him to do.

It is quite heartbreaking to realize that as things stand now, we can't get back to Eden.

So he drove out the man; and he placed at the east of the garden of Eden Cherubim, and a flaming sword which turned every way, to keep the way of the tree of life. (Genesis 3:24)

Nowhere in scripture does it say that God destroyed the garden, or somehow got rid of it. Eden is still there; we just can't see it. It is mentioned again in Revelation.

He that hath an ear, let him hear what the Spirit saith unto the churches; To him that overcometh will I give to eat of the tree of life, which is in the midst of the paradise of God. (Revelation 2:7)

The Cherubim and the flaming sword are preventing us from seeing it and entering it. And, it's just as well, because we would mess it up.

Chapter 17: Keeping our hearts

And the LORD God took the man, and put him into the garden of Eden to dress it and to keep it. (Genesis 2:15)

Eden was a place of perfect fellowship with God. Adam was supposed to keep (guard) the garden, and sadly, he failed at that task.

You and I are supposed to keep (guard) our hearts.

But take diligent heed to do the commandment and the law, which Moses the servant of the LORD charged you, to love the LORD your God, and to walk in all his ways, and to keep his commandments, and to cleave unto him, and to serve him with all your heart and with all your soul. (Joshua 22:5)

If we serve God with all our hearts, it means that our hearts are not divided. We are not serving God with part of our heart, and serving something else with another part. Our hearts are fully dedicated to loving and serving Him.

Let your heart therefore be perfect with the LORD our God, to walk in his statutes, and to keep his commandments, as at this day. (1 Kings 8:61)

Someone may ask, "How can I have a perfect heart? I'm only human. I make mistakes."

The word "perfect" in this sense means complete. Your heart and mine must be completely set aside for Him, and not for any other purpose. We see this idea of completeness in many places in the Bible.

Till we all come in the unity of the faith, and of the knowledge of the Son of God, unto a perfect man, unto the measure of the stature of the fulness of Christ: (Ephesians 4:13)

Adam was perfect. Think about it for a moment – would a perfect God create something that was not perfect? Adam was created in the image of God, Who is perfect. Adam was sinless before the fall, and he was also complete; he lacked nothing.

That the man of God may be perfect, throughly furnished unto all good works. (2 Timothy 3:17)

One way we fall short in this area is by having a divided mind and heart. As humans, we are always wandering away from Him. We serve Him with part of our heart, and another part wanders off after something else. But praise God; He always comes after His wandering sheep.

What man of you, having an hundred sheep, if he lose one of them, doth not leave the ninety and nine in the wilderness, and go after that which is lost, until he find it? (Luke 15:4)

Jesus warned us not to be divided in our thinking.

And Jesus knew their thoughts, and said unto them, Every kingdom divided against itself is brought to desolation; and every city or house divided against itself shall not stand: And if Satan cast out Satan, he is divided against himself; how shall then his kingdom stand? (Matthew 12:25-26)

James also warned us:

If any of you lack wisdom, let him ask of God, that giveth to all men liberally, and upbraideth not; and it shall be given him. But let him ask in faith, nothing wavering. For he that wavereth is like a wave of the sea driven with the wind and tossed. For let not that man think that he shall receive any thing of the Lord. A double minded man is unstable in all his ways. (James 1:5-8)

Guarding your heart involves keeping unwelcome things from entering it. If you were guarding your house, you certainly wouldn't allow a thief to come in. But it's amazing how many people allow Satan to take control of their hearts.

The thief cometh not, but for to steal, and to kill, and to destroy: I am come that they might have life, and that they might have it more abundantly. (John 10:10)

I have had to eliminate so many things from my life. These things were not necessarily evil things; they were simply distractions that were crowding into my heart, not leaving room for Him.

For example, I was having lunch with some friends, and they mentioned a certain TV program. I said that I had never seen it. We are good friends, so I didn't mind when they started poking (gentle) fun at me. I laughed along with them and said that the last time I had turned on my TV was about five months prior. This was a conscious decision I had made, because there was a certain program that I "had" to watch every week, and even though there was nothing bad about the program itself, it was a time-waster for me. The Lord had spoken to me very clearly at an earlier time that He wanted me to focus on writing books. Anyone who has ever written a book can tell you, it is a time-consuming process. You have only twenty-four hours in each day, and so do I, so how we spend those hours is very important.

I also had to eliminate spending time with certain people. These people are not evil (not more so than any other people – see Jeremiah 17:9), and the things we were doing were not evil, either, but I found myself engaging in idle chit-chat with them. After spending time with them, my heart was not renewed and replenished; it was depleted.

I have found that when I am doing what the Lord has asked me to do, even though it is very difficult, somehow, through His supernatural power, my heart is strengthened and renewed. This is most definitely the power of God working in my life; it is not my human effort or ability at work.

Take a good look at your life and your heart. Are you guarding your heart? Are you letting in only those things that God wants you to let in? If you are guarding your heart, you will have inner peace.

Be careful for nothing; but in everything by prayer and supplication with thanksgiving let your requests be made known unto God. And the peace of God, which passeth all understanding, shall keep your hearts and minds through Christ Jesus. (Philippians 4:6-7)

Mark the perfect man, and behold the upright: for the end of that man is peace. (Psalm 37:37)

Chapter 18: Lawlessness

And many false prophets shall rise, and shall deceive many. And because iniquity shall abound, the love of many shall wax cold. (Matthew 24:11-12)

Another version of this passage states, "because lawlessness shall abound, the love of many will grow cold."

We are living in a time of lawlessness. When men who are pretending to be women are granted the same rights as biological women, we are fast reaching a time when anything goes. Don't be surprised when you see these things happening:

- Children will be allowed to marry adults, because the children "identify" as adults.
- A doctor who refuses to treat a biological female for prostate cancer will be sued for malpractice.
- Pedophiles will molest children without fear of arrest, because they have the "disease" of pedophilia, and discrimination against those with diseases (any diseases) will not be tolerated.

When there is no law, it's every man for himself. When we can no longer trust our governments to create and uphold laws that protect us (and actually make sense), people's hearts will grow cold.

Many people, myself included, are disheartened by the nonsense that passes as politically correct behavior. This also happened in Bible times:

The two angels entered Sodom at sunset while Lot was sitting in the gate area of the city. When Lot saw them, he got up, greeted them, bowed low with his face to the ground, and said, "Look, my lords! Please come inside your servant's house, wash your feet, and spend the night. Then you can get up early and be on your way." But they responded, "No, we would rather spend the night in the town square." But Lot kept urging them strongly, so they turned aside and entered his house. He prepared a festival and baked unleavened flat bread for them, and they ate. Before they could lie down, all the men of Sodom and its outskirts, both young and old, surrounded the house. They called out to Lot and asked, "Where are the men who came to visit you tonight? Bring them out to us so we can have sex with them!" Lot went outside to them, shut the door behind him, and said, "I urge you, my brothers, don't do such a wicked thing. Look here, I have two daughters who are virgins. Let me bring them out to you, and you may do to them whatever you wish, only don't do anything to these men, because they're here under my protection." But they replied, "Get out of the way! This man came here as a foreigner, and now he's acting like a judge! So, we're going to deal more harshly with you than with them." Then they pushed hard against the man (that is, against Lot), intending to break down the door. But the angels inside reached out, dragged Lot back into the house with them, shut the door, and blinded the men who were at the entrance of the house, from the least important to the greatest, so they were unable to find the doorway. (Genesis 19:1-11 – International Standard Version)

Sodom was well-known as a city where homosexuality was the norm. The people who saw the angels arrive at Lot's house saw only one thing: strangers that they could take advantage of. The angels appeared in human form, as they often do throughout the Bible. Lot tried to reason with the men of Sodom, and was even willing to sacrifice his two daughters to them. If God had not supernaturally intervened by blinding them, they would have broken down the door and raped everyone in the house.

Lot tried to appease the men at his door. But listen: Satan will not be appeased. If you try to reason with him, you will be overcome by him.

Lot was willing to sacrifice his own daughters in an attempt to appease the devil. Yes, the men banging on his door were just men, but they were completely controlled by Satan.

Today, we have women being forced to sacrifice their own safety and well-being in public restrooms, changing areas and locker rooms, in order to accommodate men who are pretending to be women. We see law after law being passed which strip ordinary people of their rights, while granting special rights to those who want to practice perversion.

No one will answer this question: Why are the rights of the person who is pretending to be the opposite gender more important than the rights of the person who is not pretending?

It is more important now than ever for the believer to remain focused on Jesus Christ. The world's systems are disintegrating before our eyes, but:

I have set the LORD always before me: because he is at my right hand, I shall not be moved. (Psalm 16:8)

Don't let your heart grow cold because of the lawlessness you see all around you. You and I will never change this world through government or politics, but Jesus will transform it when he returns. Amen.

For unto us a child is born, unto us a son is given: and the government shall be upon his shoulder: and his name shall be called Wonderful, Counsellor, The mighty God, The everlasting Father, The Prince of Peace. Of the increase of his government and peace there shall be no end, upon the throne of David, and upon his kingdom, to order it, and to establish it with judgment and with justice from henceforth even forever. The zeal of the LORD of hosts will perform this. (Isaiah 9:6-7)

Chapter 19: Enduring until the end

In your patience possess ye your souls. (Luke 21:19)

The word patience is used so many times in the New Testament. In most cases it would have been better translated as "endurance."

Wherefore seeing we also are compassed about with so great a cloud of witnesses, let us lay aside every weight, and the sin which doth so easily beset us, and let us run with patience the race that is set before us. (Hebrews 12:1)

The Christian life is lived one day at a time. When going through severe trials, it is lived one hour, or even one moment at a time. If I start wondering about what awful thing is going to happen tomorrow, or next week, I will not live today for Him. I will not do today what He has asked me to do today. I will stay in bed and pull the covers over my head.

For ye have need of patience, that, after ye have done the will of God, ye might receive the promise. (Hebrews 10:36)

I have lost out on so many promises of God! He gave the promise, I received it, and I stopped right there. The verse above states, "after you have done the will of God, you...receive the promise."

There's a Christian cliché that says, "You do your part, and God will do His part." That used to make me mad. Being a believer in the partial gospel, I thought that God would do everything and I would do nothing. But the Bible says:

And ye shall be hated of all men for my name's sake: but he that endureth to the end shall be saved. (Matthew 10:22)

Endure what? Endure all the roadblocks, all the obstacles, all the negative words, and all the failures.

He also that received seed among the thorns is he that heareth the word; and the care of this world, and the deceitfulness of riches, choke the word, and he becometh unfruitful. But he that received seed into the good ground is he that heareth the word, and understandeth it; which also beareth fruit, and bringeth forth, some an hundredfold, some sixty, some thirty. (Matthew 13:22-23)

But that on the good ground are they, which in an honest and good heart, having heard the word, keep it, and bring forth fruit with patience. (Luke 8:15)

If we hear the word and understand it, and ALSO bear fruit, our souls are fertile ground for God's word to grow. When plants grow, they provide food for people. When the word of God grows in our hearts, we can then give it out to others, so they will be nourished and grow spiritually. We "bring forth fruit with patience (endurance)," as the previous verse in Luke states. Conversely, if we don't have any endurance, we're not going to bring forth any fruit.

God's part is to save us. That has to be His part, because that is something we can never do for ourselves. Our part is to hear His word, understand it, obey it, and bring forth His fruit in our lives, *with endurance.*

How many of us have never borne fruit, because when the going got tough, we gave up? When the going gets tough, we have a choice. We can either let our hearts grow cold

78

toward Him, or we can turn to Him and ask for the strength to bear some fruit.

And now also the axe is laid unto the root of the trees: therefore every tree which bringeth not forth good fruit is hewn down, and cast into the fire. (Matthew 3:10)

A good tree cannot bring forth evil fruit, neither can a corrupt tree bring forth good fruit. Every tree that bringeth not forth good fruit is hewn down, and cast into the fire. Wherefore by their fruits ye shall know them. (Matthew 7:18-20)

Jesus cursed the fig tree that didn't bear figs.

And when he saw a fig tree in the way, he came to it, and found nothing thereon, but leaves only, and said unto it, Let no fruit grow on thee henceforward forever. And presently the fig tree withered away. (Matthew 21:19).

Let's not let that happen to us, in Jesus' mighty name!

Chapter 20: Discipline

In order to endure until the end, we have to be disciplined. Discipline is needed in every area of our lives, not just one or two.

Only take heed to thyself, and keep thy soul diligently, lest thou forget the things which thine eyes have seen, and lest they depart from thy heart all the days of thy life: but teach them thy sons, and thy sons' sons; (Deuteronomy 4:9)

It is so easy for us to forget what our eyes have seen! Elijah forgot the fire that fell from heaven and consumed the sacrifice, and he forgot that he killed the false prophets (1 Kings 18:38-40). The only thing he remembered was the voice of Jezebel saying that she was going to kill him.

One way to remember what our eyes have seen is to develop good spiritual habits. This is not talked about nearly often enough in the church. Good spiritual habits require discipline.

Let's go back to the example of the athlete who wants to compete in the Olympic games. Her day may look like this:

5:00 a.m.: Wake up; run five miles
6:00 a.m.: Lift weights
7:00 a.m.: Do chin ups; drink a protein shake
8:00 a.m.: Swim two miles
9:00 a.m.: Do sit ups
10:00 a.m.: Row on the rowing machine
11:00 a.m.: Bike for three miles
12:00 p.m.: Eat lunch
1:00 p.m.: Rest
2:00 p.m.: Stretch

3:00 p.m.: Drink a protein shake
4:00 p.m.: Do MMA
5:00 p.m.: Run one mile and lift weights
6:00 p.m.: Eat dinner
7:00 p.m.: Drink a protein shake; shower
8:00 p.m.: Read a book about training for the Olympics
9:00 p.m.: Go to bed

This is a very stringent schedule! It requires a lot of discipline to adhere to. But if she does this faithfully, day after day, she has a far greater chance of making it to the Olympics than someone who simply wishes, "Gee, I sure would like to compete in the Olympics someday," and does nothing else.

In the church, we try so hard not to offend one another that we sometimes miss out on the blessings that God wants to give us. We don't want to talk too much about discipline, because someone may accuse us of being legalistic.

Question: Does anyone criticize the serious athlete for adhering to a serious schedule, so that she can attain a gold medal?

Past generations of Christians understood this. It was never questioned, or ever really even discussed. It was something that everyone knew and took for granted: If you want to mature in Christ and grow spiritually, you need to live a disciplined life.

Do you not know that those who run in a race all run, but one receives the prize? Run in such a way that you may obtain it. And everyone who competes for the prize is temperate in all things. Now they do it to obtain a perishable crown, but we for an imperishable crown. Therefore I run thus: not with uncertainty. Thus I fight: not as one who beats the air. But I discipline my body and bring it into subjection, lest, when I have preached to others, I myself should become disqualified. (1 Corinthians 9:24-27, New King James Version)

A disciplined Christian's life contains these things:

- Prayer
- Bible reading
- Taking every thought captive
- Consistent tithing and giving of offerings
- Repentance
- Forgiveness
- Counting one's blessings
- Giving thanks to God
- Witnessing to others
- Gathering often with other believers
- Reading books about the faith
- Perseverance
- Singing praises to God
- Helping those who need help

There are many other things that could be added, but this is a start.

Someone will look at this list and say that it is a bunch of rules to follow; it is legalistic, and as Christians, we are under grace, not under law. I've noticed that the Christians who talk the loudest about legalism are the ones that spend the most time watching TV and engaging in idle chit-chat. Those two items are not on the list, you'll notice.

The church today has fallen very far from where she once was. The prevalence of the partial gospel and the misuse of

God's grace has caused many people to substitute laziness for discipline.

As I stated before, there are many things that I had to eliminate from my life. The things that God wants me to do don't leave a lot of time for unnecessary things.

I have seen with my own eyes people who used to spend a lot of time in Bible reading and prayer, who now spend a lot of time in meaningless pursuits. Don't be one of them.

For the believer who wants to live a disciplined life, start small. The athlete didn't start out by running five miles; she started out by running two blocks. You can start out by reading three verses in the Bible every day, and work up to a chapter a day, or two or three. You can start out by praying for five minutes, and work up to five hours.

Satan will try to derail your efforts. This is where taking every thought captive is so important. When Satan whispered to Eve that she should eat the forbidden fruit, she should have responded with scripture and told him, "No, I can't eat fruit from that tree, because the Lord told my husband this:"

But of the tree of the knowledge of good and evil, thou shalt not eat of it: for in the day that thou eatest thereof thou shalt surely die. (Genesis 2:17)

When Satan tells you that reading your Bible is not that important, respond with this:

But he answered and said, It is written, Man shall not live by bread alone, but by every word that proceedeth out of the mouth of God. (Matthew 4:4)

When Satan lies to you and tells you that prayer doesn't work, tell him this:

If ye shall ask anything in my name, I will do it. (John 14:14)

The word of God (the Bible) is the believer's only weapon. We need to respond with scripture to every lie the devil tells us. This is what Jesus did when Satan tempted Him in the desert after He had been fasting for forty days. Satan tried to feed Jesus three different lies, and Jesus responded with three different scriptures. And guess what happened?

Then the devil left Him, and behold, angels came and ministered to Him. (Matthew 4:11, New King James Version)

I want angels to come and minister to me, don't you?

It is amazing how quickly spiritual ground can be lost, if we miss even one day of praying, reading the Bible, giving thanks, etc. Just like the Olympic hopeful will lose athletic ground if she misses training for one day, you and I will lose spiritual ground if we slack off on our spiritual disciplines for one day.

Develop good spiritual habits. Stay grounded in the word of God and in prayer. Find a church where the truth is taught and the Holy Spirit moves, and stay there.

Chapter 21: Devilish traps

Satan always lays traps for the believer. He has done this since the beginning of time, and continues to do it today. He cannot come up with any original thought, so he keeps recycling old methods.

One of Satan's tired old plots is to cause division in the church. Churches divide and split apart, often over the most trivial matters.

When I was a young and immature believer, I would sometimes get offended when I would not receive what I considered to be a proper greeting when I entered the building. Sometimes I would sit and stew about it. "I can't believe she didn't even smile at me. And I shook that man's hand, and he didn't even look at me; he was looking over my shoulder at someone else."

As I said, I was young and immature. As I got older and wiser, sometimes I was the one who was greeting people as they came in the door. I tried to make a special effort to smile at people and shake hands, but ironically, now that I was on the other end of the greeting, I noticed that some people didn't smile back at me, return my greeting, or even look at me. I was now able to overlook this, because I realized that many people are carrying a load of worry, sadness, insecurity, fear, etc., and their lack of response to me really had nothing to do with me at all.

But some people don't mature in this area. It's amazing how someone will stand and sing in church with an artificial smile on her face, all the while resenting the person next to her, because he didn't shake her hand when she came in.

May God help us. Satan loves to sow these little seeds of discord in the church. Something so trivial and unimportant can soon grow into an enormous problem.

Then said he, Unto what is the kingdom of God like? and whereunto shall I resemble it? It is like a grain of mustard seed, which a man took, and cast into his garden; and it grew, and waxed a great tree; and the fowls of the air lodged in the branches of it. (Luke 13:18-19)

"Fowls of the air" in the Bible often refer to demonic spirits. See Matthew 13:4, Mark 4:4, Luke 8:5, Revelation 19:17, 21. If we give Satan a foothold in the church, by becoming offended over something someone did or said to us (or failed to do or say), we open the door for demonic spirits to come in and make themselves at home.

Remember, the church is not a building. The church is you and me. Don't let demonic spirits come and make themselves at home in the church.

Be on the alert for devilish traps. Satan loves to carry stories from one person to another. If someone starts talking about someone else, and the other person is not there, that is gossip, and that is a trap. Don't fall into the trap! Politely excuse yourself from that conversation and find something else to do. If it keeps happening, you will need to confront the person and say something like, "I don't feel comfortable talking about her when she's not here." Sometimes that's all it takes to silence the gossip.

The Bible has a lot to say about this.

Where no wood is, there the fire goeth out: so where there is no talebearer, the strife ceaseth. (Proverbs 26:20)

A froward man soweth strife: and a whisperer separateth chief friends. (Proverbs 16:28)

I saw this happen in my hometown church, and it was heartbreaking. Person A said something negative about person B, and person A and B were very good friends. Person C went to person B and told him what person A had said about him. Person B became upset and confronted person A. Person A was not a mature Christian; rather than confessing and asking person B to forgive him, he became indignant and stubborn about it. Their friendship was effectively ruined. Person C should have repented of being a tale-bearer and asked the other two to forgive him, but he didn't, so it ended in tragedy with person A leaving the church, and persons B and C having a strained relationship. Satan set the whole thing up, and no one was mature enough or wise enough to repent, ask forgiveness, and move forward.

Gossip, a lack of empathy for others, refusing to ask for forgiveness, and stubbornness are all signs of a cold heart. When we have done wrong and refuse to do anything about it, it means we don't fear God.

And the man said, The woman whom thou gavest to be with me, she gave me of the tree, and I did eat. (Genesis 3:12)

Adam fell into the trap of blaming someone else for his problem. Blaming someone else for what you did wrong will not lessen your negative consequences; it will increase them.

Many things can and do go wrong in the church. Sometimes it is necessary to get to the bottom of things and sort out who did what, but sometimes, it's not. Sometimes the best thing you and I can do is admit there is a problem, repent of any involvement we may have had in it, and even if we had nothing to do with it, ask God for healing for everyone involved, grace to forgive, peace of mind and soul, and the ability to move forward.

The church is God's expression of Himself here on earth. Isn't she worth sacrificing for?

Also of your own selves shall men arise, speaking perverse things, to draw away disciples after them. Therefore watch, and remember, that by the space of three years I ceased not to warn every one night and day with tears. (Acts 20:30-31)

The apostle Paul was warning the believers that people would enter the church and try to pull people out of the church. He saw the devilish trap that Satan was laying for these people, and he wanted them to avoid it.

A prudent man foreseeth the evil, and hideth himself: but the simple pass on, and are punished. (Proverbs 22:3)

Remember, Satan wants to destroy you and me.

To whom ye forgive anything, I forgive also: for if I forgave anything, to whom I forgave it, for your sakes forgave I it in the person of Christ; Lest Satan should get an advantage of us: for we are not ignorant of his devices. (2 Corinthians 2:10-11)

Adam and Eve were not alert to the danger, and they fell into Satan's trap. Don't let Satan use you to further his agenda. Be on the lookout for his traps, so you don't fall in.

Chapter 22: The tree of life

And out of the ground made the LORD God to grow every tree that is pleasant to the sight, and good for food; the tree of life also in the midst of the garden, and the tree of knowledge of good and evil. (Genesis 2:9)

And the LORD God commanded the man, saying, Of every tree of the garden thou mayest freely eat: But of the tree of the knowledge of good and evil, thou shalt not eat of it: for in the day that thou eatest thereof thou shalt surely die. (Genesis 2:16-17)

Adam and Eve were told not to eat from the tree of knowledge of good and evil. What is this tree? What does it symbolize? And why did God put it there?

I believe the tree of knowledge of good and evil symbolizes God, Himself.

Such knowledge is too wonderful for me; it is high, I cannot attain unto it. (Psalm 139:6)

We cannot access God by ourselves. We are sinful, and God is sinless. It is His mercy to us that He doesn't appear to us, because if He did, we would be reduced to ashes.

And he (God) said, Thou canst not see my face: for there shall no man see me, and live. (Exodus 33:20)

What is the tree of life? What does it symbolize? And why did God put it in the garden of Eden?

The tree of life is Jesus Christ, Himself.

Jesus saith unto him, I am the way, the truth, and the life: no man cometh unto the Father, but by me. (John 14:6)

Adam and Eve had the opportunity to eat the fruit from the tree of life, but they didn't.

And the LORD God commanded the man, saying, Of every tree of the garden thou mayest freely eat: (Genesis 2:16)

The tree of life was included in "every tree of the garden" that God told Adam and Eve to freely eat from. We can only speculate as to why they didn't.

Human nature really doesn't change very much. How many times has God asked you or me to do something, and we don't do it? Here are the reasons we give:

- I'm afraid to do that; I've never done it before.
- I don't know how to do that.
- What if something goes wrong?
- I'm not qualified to do that.
- There are other people who can do that better than I can.
- I'm tired; I'll do it later.
- It's too hard.
- I don't want to.

I wonder if the reason why Adam and Eve didn't eat from the tree of life was one of the above.

God determines good and evil. He decides what is sinful and what is not.

I form the light, and create darkness: I make peace, and create evil: I the LORD do all these things. (Isaiah 45:7)

Eating from the tree of knowledge of good and evil caused Adam and Eve to become their own gods. They would now be the ones to determine good and evil, and decide what was right and what was wrong. By their sin, they took the authority out of God's hands and put it in their own hands.

And the LORD God said, Behold, the man is become as one of us, to know good and evil: (Genesis 3:22a)

Simply knowing good and evil isn't the issue. Deciding what is good and evil is the issue. You and I don't have the omniscience that God has to determine what is right and what is wrong. In order to judge correctly in every situation, we would need to have all the knowledge about every situation, and we never do. That's why God has given us clear guidelines in the Bible about right and wrong, good and evil. If it was up to you and me to decide, we would make the wrong decision.

If you doubt this, look around at the world today. We have people making laws and decisions that are absolutely asinine. Why? Because our governments have taken God out of the equation. If you don't want God involved in your decision-making, you will come up with laws that say it's okay to murder an unborn baby, or a baby that has already been born, but is unwanted. You will say that it's okay to pretend to be the opposite gender of the one you were born as, and make laws protecting people who want to do that. You will say that it's okay to stage violent protests and destroy property, but it's not okay to attend church.

...and now, lest he put forth his hand, and take also of the tree of life, and eat, and live forever: (Genesis 3:22b)

God sent Adam out of Eden, and blocked the entrance with an angel who had a flaming sword.

I read a commentary on this topic. The writer said that God didn't want Adam and Eve to eat the fruit from the tree of life after they had eaten from the tree of knowledge of good and evil, because they would then live forever in their physical bodies, in their sinful state, eternally separated from God, with no way back to Him. So, it was God's mercy to send Adam out of Eden.

Before the fall, Adam and Eve were sinless. If they had eaten of the tree of life, they would have lived forever, sinless. I believe this was God's intention for them. But after they sinned, death started working in their bodies immediately.

...for in the day that thou eatest thereof thou shalt surely die. (Genesis 2:17b)

The literal translation of this reads: in the day that you eat of it, dying, you shall die. And it was true. Adam and Eve died before reaching one thousand years of age. They died in "the day" they ate the fruit.

But, beloved, be not ignorant of this one thing, that one day is with the Lord as a thousand years, and a thousand years as one day. (2 Peter 3:8)

After the fall, Adam and Eve were sinners, and all their children were sinners, and every person ever born on this planet was born a sinner, except Jesus Christ.

And almost all things are by the law purged with blood; and without shedding of blood is no remission. (Hebrews 9:22)

For this is my blood of the new testament, which is shed for many for the remission of sins. (Matthew 26:28)

Jesus took your sin and mine upon Himself when He died on the cross. By receiving the sacrifice that He made for us, we can live forever with Him in heaven, in a sinless state. He had to shed His blood first, before that could happen.

Before the fall, it would have been no problem for Adam and Eve to eat from the tree of life and live forever. They didn't have any sin. After the fall, in order for them to be forgiven, a sacrifice had to be made.

Unto Adam also and to his wife did the LORD God make coats of skins, and clothed them. (Genesis 3:21)

At least two animals gave their lives so that Adam and Eve could be covered. This is the first blood sacrifice recorded in the Bible.

Jesus Christ is the tree of life. There must have been something awesome about that tree in the garden, something mysterious, something solemn, which made Adam and Eve hesitate to approach it.

Someone is saying, "How can Jesus be a tree? That's silly."

Jesus is described as many different things in the Bible, including a tree. Here are some:

- A door (John 10:9a)
- A pearl (Matthew 13:46)
- Bread (John 6:48)
- Seed (Luke 8:11)

- A stone (Matthew 21:42)
- A lamb (John 1:29)
- A bridegroom (Matthew 25:6)
- Light (John 1:9)
- The word of God (John 1:1)
- The prize (Philippians 3:14)
- A sword (Ephesians 6:17)
- Water (John 4:10)
- A lion (Revelation 5:5)
- A street[1] (Revelation 21:21, 22:2)
- A tree (Revelation 22:2)

Whoso eateth my flesh, and drinketh my blood, hath eternal life; and I will raise him up at the last day. (John 6:54)

If we make Jesus Christ a part of us, described metaphorically as eating His flesh and drinking His blood, we will have eternal life, and we will be raised up at the last day.

Everything we do in our physical bodies on this earth is incomplete. We make Jesus a part of us, but we do so only partially. If we overcome our sins – the world, the flesh, and the devil – we will partake of Him fully in His kingdom.

He that hath an ear, let him hear what the Spirit saith unto the churches; To him that overcometh will I give to eat of the tree of life, which is in the midst of the paradise of God. (Revelation 2:7)

The word "paradise" is a word that we think is synonymous with heaven. But it means "garden."

In the midst of the street of it, and on either side of the river, was there the tree of life, which bare twelve manner of fruits, and yielded her fruit every month: and the leaves of the tree were for the healing of the nations. (Revelation 22:2)

In Jesus' kingdom here on earth, we see Jesus as the street (the "way"), Jesus as the river (living water), and Jesus as the tree of life. The Bible uses very descriptive language to show us Jesus the street, leading us to Jesus the water, out of which Jesus the tree is growing. It is a beautiful picture.

Blessed are they that do his commandments, that they may have right to the tree of life, and may enter in through the gates into the city. (Revelation 22:14)

Jesus said, *"...my yoke is easy, and My burden is light." (Matthew 11:30)* When we do His commandments, He will give us His divine power to carry them out. No matter what He has asked of us, His grace is sufficient for us to do whatever He has called us to do. He will then reward us with Himself, the tree of life.

1. Note: Despite what you may have heard about "streets of gold" in heaven, there is no reference to this in the Bible. There is A STREET of gold (Jesus Christ), the way through the city of God, the people of God, the bride of Christ, New Jerusalem. See Revelation 21:21. Jesus Christ is THE WAY – the only way (John 14:6).

Chapter 23: God calling

And they heard the voice of the LORD God walking in the garden in the cool of the day: and Adam and his wife hid themselves from the presence of the LORD God amongst the trees of the garden. And the LORD God called unto Adam, and said unto him, Where art thou? (Genesis 3:8-9)

And the LORD said unto Cain, Where is Abel thy brother? (Genesis 4:9a)

And the LORD came, and stood, and called as at other times, Samuel, Samuel. Then Samuel answered, Speak; for thy servant heareth. (1 Samuel 3:10)

Also I heard the voice of the Lord, saying, Whom shall I send, and who will go for us? Then said I, Here am I; send me. (Isaiah 6:8)

As believers we have the holy privilege of hearing God's voice and doing His will. Adam and Eve hid from the voice of God. Cain became belligerent when God asked him a question. Samuel, at first, did not know that God was speaking to him; he thought it was Eli. But Eli gave him the right words to say in response to God's call. Isaiah told the Lord that he was available to go wherever God chose to send him.

In each of these cases, God knew the answer to the question he was asking. He knew Adam was hiding in the trees; He knew Cain had killed his brother; He knew Samuel was just an inexperienced child, yet called to him anyway to give him a word of prophecy, and He knew that Isaiah was the one He would send.

God asks us questions, not because He doesn't know the answer and He is seeking information from us. No! He asks us questions so that the condition of our own hearts will be revealed to us.

When Adam and Eve heard God calling, their hearts' condition was revealed. They were in the "cool of the day." Their life spans, symbolized as a "day," had been cut short, and they had moved from the warmth and beauty of God's presence to the coldness of separation from Him. The moment they ate the fruit that God had told them not to eat, they died spiritually, and they began to die physically. Even though they lived for hundreds of years after that, their lives were on a downward path to death.

God never intended for you and me to die. He never intended for animals or plants to die. Death comes from Satan; life comes from God.

The thief cometh not, but for to steal, and to kill, and to destroy: I am come that they might have life, and that they might have it more abundantly. (John 10:10)

For if by one man's offence death reigned by one; much more they which receive abundance of grace and of the gift of righteousness shall reign in life by one, Jesus Christ. (Romans 5:17)

Cain replied angrily when God asked him where Abel was. When we have done wrong and refuse to do anything about it, it means we don't fear God. I believe Cain was banished, not because he murdered Abel, but because he refused to repent for what he'd done.

Thankfully, Samuel and Isaiah responded to God's call positively, and God blessed them.

97

What has God called you to do? No matter what it is, obey Him.

God usually doesn't call us to do easy things. Remember the athlete? Ask Him to help you. He will.

Saying, Father, if thou be willing, remove this cup from me: nevertheless not my will, but thine, be done. (Luke 22:42)

Jesus' task was the hardest anyone has ever had to face, but He did it.

Chapter 24: Abundant life

Eden was bursting with life. Every plant, every tree, every type of vegetation was alive in the fullest sense, far beyond the life as we know it that plants have today. I believe that Adam spoke to the grass and it obeyed him; he spoke to the trees and they obeyed him.

God wants you and me to have that same kind of life. Even though we are made of dirt, we have the capability to hear God's voice and to obey Him. What a privilege!

For he knoweth our frame; he remembereth that we are dust. (Psalm 103:14)

Sometimes when I get impatient with myself, I remind myself that I am dust. Believe me, it helps! You and I are to live a life of faith, looking to Him for everything, because we know we are only dust.

I am crucified with Christ: nevertheless I live; yet not I, but Christ liveth in me: and the life which I now live in the flesh I live by the faith of the Son of God, who loved me, and gave himself for me. (Galatians 2:20)

This verse in Galatians is one of my favorites. My old life has been crucified, with its affections and lusts, and it has been exchanged for His new life, with its beauty and purpose.

And they that are Christ's have crucified the flesh with the affections and lusts. (Galatians 5:24)

And to her was granted that she should be arrayed in fine linen, clean and white: for the fine linen is the righteousness of saints. (Revelation 19:8)

It is so beautiful to know that in spite of my sin, in spite of the fact that I am just dust, in spite of all my failures and problems, Jesus Christ has clothed me with His righteousness and enabled me to stand blameless before Him.

For in him dwelleth all the fulness of the Godhead bodily. And ye are complete in him, which is the head of all principality and power: (Colossians 2:9-10)

Jesus Christ offers everything you and I need to live an abundant life. We are complete in Him, not because of anything we have done or anything we are, but because He has made us complete.

If you long for Eden, as I do, there is one way back. If you have received Jesus Christ as your savior, you will have a spot reserved there.

He that hath an ear, let him hear what the Spirit saith unto the churches; To him that overcometh will I give to eat of the tree of life, which is in the midst of the paradise of God. (Revelation 2:7)

If you have never received Jesus as your savior, take this opportunity and pray right now:

"Jesus, I know I'm a sinner. I know I cannot access heaven on my own. I ask You to come into my heart and my life, and give me a new heart and a new life. From this day forward, I dedicate my life to serving You. I know You will help me to stand through every impossible circumstance, and give me the strength to endure to the end. From this day forward, the old is gone, and the new has come. In Your mighty name, amen."

The Bible says:

For whosoever shall call upon the name of the Lord shall be saved. (Romans 10:13)

Call upon His name.

Wherefore he is able also to save them to the uttermost that come unto God by him, seeing he ever liveth to make intercession for them. (Hebrews 7:25)

I pray that you have been blessed by this book. May I see you in Eden someday!

The LORD bless thee, and keep thee: The LORD make his face shine upon thee, and be gracious unto thee: The LORD lift up his countenance upon thee, and give thee peace. (Numbers 6:24-26)

Amen.

Julia Anshasi
2020

www.ingramcontent.com/pod-product-compliance
Lightning Source LLC
Chambersburg PA
CBHW021152090426
42740CB00008B/1057